A JOURNEY IN FAITH

Along the Spiritual Highway

William S. Johnson

Publisher
Fairway Press

A Journey In Faith

FIRST EDITION
Copyright © 1995 by
William S. Johnson

Library of Congress Catalog Card Number: 95-94665

ISBN 0-7880-0622-3

PRINTED IN U.S.A.

This book is dedicated to

Jesus Christ, my Lord and Savior, that this humble effort may in some small way serve Him and bring glory to His name,

With special appreciation to

My dear family: Yvonne, Bruce, Michael and Stephanie who were so supportive and continually encouraging; and without their love and sharing, this book would not have been possible.

Table of Contents

Foreword

Why this book

It was a cool and foreboding afternoon that late summer day some twenty years ago. As I sat on the balcony of our condominium, I looked out over the turbulent Atlantic Ocean. Somewhere beyond the horizon a summer storm was playing with the elements of nature. The sky was a dark gray, but there were streaks of orange that told of a sun off in the distance that could do no more than reflect its light. The sun's warmth had already given way to the ever thickening cloud cover. The sea was rushing toward the shore with forceful waves of ten feet and more. White glistening sand was giving way to the strong undertow, just as the lounging sun worshippers and playful swimmers had given way to the sense of the coming storm.

But in all this fury and change, a peace came over me that I had never known before. I knew that God was at work within me just as He was at work with the natural elements around me. My thoughts drifted back to happy memories as well as reminders of the turmoil of my life. Then my thoughts went forward to what was yet to be experienced. I saw grand things for my family and me. It seemed that we had only happy times ahead in calm seas. How naive of me.

Then a desire to write a book sprang from within me. Not one book, but a trilogy. I envisioned writing about the experiences of our family to share with others. In my mind I saw the book titles: Family Founding, Family Force, Family Faith. I would graphically explain the growth of our faith and the nurturing of the spiritual growth of our children. All the answers to one's stormy life were forming in my mind through the family experiences we had and were to have. Little did I know then that what seemed to be a lifetime of experiences was but a brief chapter in the book of life. Even with my active imagination, I could not

possibly have foreseen all that was before my family. The big
storms were still off in the distance. How could I have possibly
known then that I had few answers? I didn't even know the
questions.

The energies of that young adult have given way to the realities
of this aging man. My book will be less than I dreamed, but the
message remains the same: to still the stormy seas in our life.

Before we begin

The comments and compilations presented in this work are
neither extreme fundamentalist nor extreme liberal in content.
There is no intent in being "the middle of the road". I am but a
layman. The expressions on these pages are not from a theolo-
gian, philosopher, psychologist, physicist or evangelist. These
are the thoughts, experiences and perceptions of one who holds
Jesus at the center of his life. You are about to be given a
generous dose of "Johnsonism".

This book is a compilation of what I will call a travel guide. It is
a guide of a journey taken by our family: a journey in faith,
toward the truth. Along the way there will be many stops
resulting in short presentations of basic concepts of the Christian
faith and my beliefs concerning them. It is not an attempt to
present a full discussion of the subjects covered, but rather to
give a reference point from which to mark one's journey toward
understanding. Consider these as milestones along your way, or
street signs along the road you travel. It is up to the traveler to
stop where they may to further explore the wonders beyond the
marker, to visit the houses along the street.

The subjects are generously supported by Bible passages. Where
I have used direct quotes, I have elected the NIV translation.
The biblical references are not all encompassing, but are the
passages in which I have found special meaning.

How to use this guide

These presentations were developed over a period of time to help someone that I was discipling in grasping the essence of their faith so they may realize a personal relationship with Jesus. They were written in love for that person and in my love of God. Each one of the fifty subjects may be reviewed separately. Although I have placed an order to the subjects, they do not have to be reviewed in that particular order and each subject should stand on its own. You should find, though, that the subjects are in harmony, one with the other.

Each subject contains a graphic, i.e., a diagram, chart or table, that is intended to give a quick perception and review of the concept. The text before the graphic is intended to give an introduction to the concept and show application through my personal experience or some related readings. Text immediately before and/or following the graphic is a further refinement within my understanding of the concept. Biblical references are provided to encourage additional study. It should be emphasized that every attempt is made to keep the references within the context of the subject matter. Further insight into the meaning of the text can be obtained by reading a number of preceding and succeeding verses.

Look at each subject as a milestone. At the end of the discussion, the milestone is presented as a brief statement of action that the traveler can take. With that milestone is listed a few questions to enable the individual, or travel group, to explore beyond the milestone. Consider these questions as thought, or discussion, stimulators. See if you see what I see. May the Lord lead you along the paths He would have you walk.

These are not complete studies on the subjects; that is for someone else to do, if indeed that is humanly possible. Even though you make a journey with a companion, the perceptions of what you pass are different as are the expectations of the destination.

You truly travel alone on your journey toward the truth.

I leave you my thoughts. These thoughts are not necessarily original, but you will find the organization and graphic presentations are unique. Consider the material as thought stimulators for the formation of your own beliefs. Enjoy the stories of my walk with God. I pray that you will find this helpful as God strives to reveal Himself more fully to you.

Introduction

The Thought Process

My older son, Bruce, is a deep thinker. He approaches everything with the disciplined logic of a scientist. When he came to many of the crossroads in his life, Bruce succumbed to "paralysis by analysis" as he researched for the right answers. Recently, he told me that he would like to share in my walk with God but he didn't know how. I rejoiced at the opportunity to share Jesus with him, but I knew I would have to present this to Bruce in a manner that would appeal to his sense of logic. We began our walk together by discussing some of the scientific theories about life. Believe me when I say that I am in way over my head in this area. This chapter presents some of the thoughts that we shared as we looked for a springboard into the biblical truths.

Since the very creation of human beings, God has given each individual an awareness of God. The root of this understanding is the same in every individual that has ever lived on this earth, or who will ever live on this earth. Building on that awareness, God continues to reveal Himself to each of us in doses that He knows we can absorb. It is the God-created uniqueness in each individual that expresses what they know of God. The awareness, expression, contemplation and knowing of God has varied across time, but the basic truth of God is always the same.

How do we think about the "truth of God"? My limited searching into the scientific world for an answer to this question brings to me the realization that personal experience, language and time become barriers to the human knowledge of the Ultimate Truth (God). I see the limitations of my humanness as keeping me from knowing this truth.

To briefly touch on each of these barriers, I have the following comments:

> **Personal experience** — The body of our experience is made up of the education we have obtained, our sensory perceptions, and our participation in fellowship. It is from this that all our thoughts and actions are measured. Even to imagine an experience not yet known must be done through what we have known.

> **Language** — Thinking is not restricted by the limitations of language, but the expression of our thinking is so restricted. To name and define something that is thought about gives that thought identity and structure. But even at that, the expression of that thought will be interpreted by someone else based on their own perceptions of the meaning of the expression.

> **Time** — The human concept of time can distort thought. The time of the reality of the occurrence is not, necessarily, the same as the time of the meaning of the occurrence. There is an identity of the subject as it relates to a difference in time just as there is an identity of time as it relates to a difference in the subject.

The following table presents what I understand to be the phases of thinking. It is up to the individual to position themself within the appropriate phase regarding the subject being thought about. Understand that thinking is a process and each individual moves through the process at the pace they set for themselves.

Four Phases of Thinking

Pre Thought	Literal Thought	Reflective Thought	After Thought
Awareness	Expression	Contemplation	Knowing
Conception	Presentation	Projection	Donation
Experience of awareness without definition	Experience of logical or sensational objects	Experience of phenomena or depth	Experience of creativity
No distinction between thinking and being or subject and object (Dreamstate)	Thinking of objects by conscious subjects (Corresponding); no distinction between reality, truth, meaning	Distinction between meaning and reality; a division of the true from the untrue (Reflective)	Recognition of truth and the depth of truth carried to the Ultimate Truth (Responsive)
No perception of reality	Reality is found in an appearance that senses perception as interpreted in language	Reality is modified by bringing meaning to the experience	Meaning is modified by bringing truth to the experience in relation to the understanding of time

Primitive humans had an awareness of God. Their expression of that can be found in archeological discoveries of stone and earthen mounds reaching to the heavens, the cave paintings of the Cro-Magnon Man depicting supernatural intervention, and evidence of early-man reverently burying their dead. Ancient Assyrian and Egyptian writings contain concepts of God and eternal life that we now hold as doctrine. Greek and Roman mythology present highly imaginative stories that reflect the workings of God. The awareness was there in the beginning. An ability to express that awareness was made easier with the development of the spoken and written word, language. As people contemplated the expressed beliefs, these beliefs were stylized. All of these steps lead us on our journey toward the truth.

God reveals Himself to us in a manner that humans are prepared to accept. Can I differentiate what is symbolically real and what is abstractly correct? The Bible is a book of truth. It is God's revelation of Himself to us. God has not changed, man has!

Only God is all-knowing. On my travel toward the truth, I can become more knowing. With the talents He has entrusted to me, I can be creative in applying those gifts. That will allow me to serve Him by giving back, donating, to society the use of those talents. In that, I will find meaning in my life by serving others.

Milestone #1

Allow awareness to become knowing.

1. Why is it difficult for most individuals to express their feelings and awareness?

2. Explain a recent situation where you believe you were misunderstood. Why did you feel misunderstood?

3. Read 2 Peter 3:1-2. What does Peter recommend to stimulate wholesome thinking? How would you apply this?

4. Have you read any stories about the workings of god(s), other than what is in the Bible? Describe. Are there any elements of similarity between these stories and any biblical stories? Explain.

5. How would you go about searching for an answer on a particular worrisome problem?

6. Is it possible to become fully knowledgeable on a particular subject? Consider the impact of changes in environment and time. How does this impact your beliefs?

Life Cycle

Sigmund Freud has often been called the father of psychology. For it was he that set a framework, a structure, for what we know as modern psychology. A student of the Freudian School, Erik Erikson, modified and expanded the model of the stages in a person's life cycle. More on this later.

Long before Freud, the Bible acknowledged the life cycles in man and woman as it relates to spiritual growth. In the book of Psalms (1:1), we have the life cycle, or progression of the unfaithful. "Blessed is the man who does not walk in the counsel of the wicked, or stand in the way of sinners, or sit in the seat of mockers." It brings to mind the first steps of the infant, where walk refers to the wicked. Then, the firm standing of the young, where stand refers to the sinners. Then, the need for the elders to sit, where sit refers to the mockers. The way of the unbeliever then is to be tempted, to succumb to the ways of temptation, and then to scoff at those who do not.

Another example of a life cycle comes from the New Testament. It reflects on the life cycle of the faithful.

Growth in the Believer
1 John 1:12-14

Stage	Verse	Text	Condition
Children	12	your sins have been forgiven on account of his name	Forgiven
	13	you have known the Father.	Aware
Young Men	13	you have overcome the evil one	Tempted
	14	you are strong and the word of God lives in you	Righteous
Fathers	13	you have known him who is from the beginning	Knowing
	14	you have known him who is from the beginning	Mature

As a believer, we move from the awareness of the forgiveness of sins, to overcoming temptation and selfishness, to imparting spiritual truth. I think it is noteworthy that the fathers have to be reminded they are knowing and mature. It implies the responsibility to impart that knowledge.

As I reviewed this passage, I recalled the occasion that I first realized the major life cycles we all go through. It was the first birthday of our grandson, Ryan. As I thought of him and the year since his birth, my mind raced back to the birth of his father, my son Michael. I then mentally scanned all the years in between. From that reflection, I wrote a letter to Ryan. A letter I knew he could not yet read, but a letter I knew I had to write. Following are excerpts from that letter:

> "It has been one year since you have started your grand adventure in life. And what an adventure it is! There are no pathways prepared for you as you venture forth. But you will have within you the capabilities to make your own way. My dear Grandson, your life will be what you make it.

> "You are fortunate, however, that you need not walk the pathways of life alone. With you, always, will be your parents — encouraging, directing, sharing in your adventures. At times they will also be disciplinarians. But this will be out of their love to guide you away from dangers and misdirections that they have witnessed and experienced. Do not ever doubt their love for you and their concern for your well being....

> "It was not too long ago that your father started his adventure. While to me it seems like yesterday, the calendar tells me it has been nearly three decades. As I look back, many, many fond memories race through my mind. You see, as a son, your father made it easy for me to be a part of his life. He is, most certainly, a large part

of my life. The sharing of good times and bad times, laughter and tears, strengths and weaknesses, has made us both stronger. And while our ventures take us down different pathways, we are always close. What now seems to be just moments of sharing have given me a lifetime of memories that no one can erase....

"Accept my belief in the Almighty God and the Christian doctrine. For surely, the miracle of birth, the joy of a father and son relationship, is a blessing from the Supreme Being that is beyond the comprehension of man. The morality of this faith will make your adventure less stressful. It is through a strong and committed belief that you will be blessed and, through you, others will be blessed. It is through faith that we obtain the optimism and hope for tomorrow. It is through hope that we obtain love for all. It is through love we strengthen our faith....

"Follow the precepts of your father, for he will not disappoint you. He has never disappointed me. Strange how the responsibility of father to son becomes the responsibility of son to father. As a father, I never expected it to happen, but it did. When did it happen? I cannot answer this question. The change evolved gradually, but I suspect it started when your father was at an early age. For it was through his love, strength, conviction and common sense that he took charge. It is because of this that he will hold your family together. It is a great comfort to me to know how capable your father will be as the cornerstone of your family.

"Today you will not understand the meaning of these words, just as yesterday I would not have. But tomorrow you will know what I am meagerly trying to explain. The words themselves are nothing; it is the heartfelt feeling that yearns to express itself. Can I now say to you what I have been reluctant to say to my son, your father?....

"Know always that I deeply love you and I want to be the extension of your father. While I may not be at your side, I will be with you each and every step along your pathway of life. Reach out and I'll take your hand. Ask and I'll counsel you. Cry out and I'll comfort you. Laugh and I'll share in your joys."

This became a letter that I couldn't write to my son, that my father could not write to me. Yet the message is known by all the parties. While my earthly father did not write such a letter, my heavenly Father did. It is an open letter to all. It is the Bible.

Now back to the life cycles accepted in modern psychology. I am not qualified to explain them, nor defend them. However, I found it interesting that the life cycle is separated into eight stages of psycho/social growth.

Eight Stages of Psycho/Social and Spiritual Growth

"Therefore, let us teach the elementary teachings about Christ and go on to maturity..." (Hebrews 6:1)

Psycho/Social Growth			Spiritual Growth Matthew 5	
Stage	**Age**	**Virtue**	**Condition**	**Verse**
Trust vs. Mistrust	1st year	Hope	Spiritual poverty	3
Autonomy vs. Self-doubt	2-3 years	Will	Mournful	4
Initiative vs. Guilt	3-4 years	Purpose	Humble	5
Industry vs. Inferiority	School years	Competence	Desire to be right	6
Identity vs. Diffusion	Adolescence	Fidelity	Compassionate	7
Intimacy vs. Isolation	Young adult	Love	Pure in heart	8
Generativity vs. Stagnation	Adult	Care	Peacemaker	9
Integrity vs. Despair	Old age	Wisdom	Persecuted	10

This is certainly more than the three stages I presented earlier, but it is in line with the eight stages of spiritual growth that the Lord addressed in the Sermon on the Mount, more specifically, the Beatitudes. While they may not exactly match-up, there is a remarkable similarity in the attributes of the psycho/social and spiritual growth stages. From the Beatitudes, "Blessed" means to be made happy by God. Let's just follow the growth steps to that ultimate happiness.

- The poor in spirit are those who put their whole trust in God, for He is their hope.

- The mournful are those who have seen suffering and who have acknowledged their sin; they have the will to go on for they know they will be comforted.

- The meek are those who are humble before God and others as they are aware of their real purpose in life.

- Those who hunger and thirst for righteousness are those who want to be right with God; they strive for greater competence in wholeheartedness.

- The merciful are those who show compassion; who through their own self-identity can display fidelity to others.

- The pure in heart are those who have no lust within them and who give love to all.

- The peacemakers are those who do not have a divisive spirit and through an attitude of care, strive to reconcile all to God's ways.

- The persecuted are those who have faced hardships and met the opposition; through their faithfulness they have gained the wisdom to share with others.

Growth, psycho/social or spiritual, brings a steady progression in ethical behavior. While the stages in the psycho/social growth are shown as conflicts in positive and negative attributes, the stages in spiritual growth are presented with the results of that growth development, i.e., those that mourn will be comforted, the meek will inherit, the merciful will be shown mercy, etc.

The basic point to make here is that ethics is not the avoidance of conflict with the moral ideal, but rather the capacity to provide righteous strength in the actual conduct of individuals. Ethical action enhances virtue in oneself and creates virtue in others. The source of that ethical action, the righteous life, is the natural goodness that God has given each of us. But that goodness needs nurturing.

As I see it, spirituality (morality) is knowing righteousness; ethics (virtue as defined by society and/or psychologists) is acting in a righteous manner; truth (purity) is being wholly righteous. Since I define God as the ultimate, or pure, truth, I envision a process of travelling toward that truth. God gives us, at the conception of life, the knowledge of right and wrong; this is our spirituality. We work at defining and redefining that awareness to suit our desires, pride and greed. This becomes the socially acceptable ethics. God then needs to reveal again the truth of right and wrong; this He may do individually or more globally. The process has come full circle, but it is a continuum and it goes on and on.

Milestone #2

Enable spiritual poverty to mature to spiritual sharing.

1. The Sermon on the Mount (Matthew 5-7) speaks to the need for a new life through spiritual growth. What does it mean to be poor in spirit (Matthew 5:3)? Refer to Revelations 2:8-11, 3:14-20.

2. Describe the last time you were really happy. Has anyone given you advice for happiness? What was that advice? Being comforted for the intense sorrow of one's spiritual condition (Matthew 5:4) will bring happiness.

3. What does it mean to have personal humility (Matthew 5:5)?

4. Spiritual poverty, sorrow over sin, and personal humility are man's need. The solution to that need is the desire to be right (Matthew 5:6). How would you describe your desire to be right? What does being right mean to you?

5. The results of being a citizen of the Kingdom of God are showing mercy to others (Matthew 5:7), being pure in heart (Matthew 5:8), and being a peacemaker (Matthew 5:9). How are these results reflected in your life?

6. What is your greatest potential source, or reason, of persecution as a Christian? Examine the following and discuss how persecution may come to you:

    John 17:14
    Acts 4:16-20, 5:29, 5:40-42
    1 Corinthians 4:9-12
    2 Corinthians 12:10
    2 Timothy 2:9-12

Theory of Relativity

As a child growing up in an inner-city environment, I was rather small, frail and timid. I truly was a push-over for the bigger boys with whom I tried to associate. Many an afternoon I would come home with a bloody nose and assorted scrapes and bruises. Sometimes, the walk home from school seemed to take forever as the other boys would torment me. Through elementary school and into junior high, I was considered small for my age. This coupled with the fact that I was generally the youngest one in the class compounded the problem.

Shortly after we moved into the suburbs, I had a sudden growth spurt. Within three or four months I found that I had caught up with my classmates in size and in fact became one of the taller boys in the class. I still carried with me a "small" attitude though. I had always been aggressive in my studies and that continued, but so did the timidness in my relationship with other boys.

In about the ninth grade, I became more active in team sports. As my participation in these sports increased, I grew in strength and ability. This led to some level of confidence in being able to hold my own against most anyone. Then later that year, the high school football coach asked me to try out for the team. I never played real football before, only the sandlot style that was more than touch football.

I was surprised to find myself actually trying out for the team. It seemed all the boys there were so much older, bigger, stronger and capable. However, I was determined to see this through. In my own mind, I assumed that I would be dropped before the season would ever get off the ground. Somehow I survived the last cut and made the team. The memory of that moment is still very clear in my mind. My self-talk was, "Well you made the team; now let's see if you can make the starting lineup."

Practice intensified as we prepared for the opening game of the season. I was filling-in in the defensive backfield. On one particular play, the senior fullback broke through the line of scrimmage and came charging down the field toward me. Momentarily I froze. But then I started charging the fullback, somewhat realizing that there was going to be a big collision and I was going to be left in the dirt. It made me concentrate more and charge even harder. There was a collision. But the big fullback was on the ground and he got up limping. And I felt good. In my panic I had earned a spot on the starting lineup, but also I learned a lesson in the sport: The harder you tackle a bigger player, the less likely you are to get hurt. The reason for this is simple. It is supported by one of the theorems of physics: Force equals mass times velocity. In other words, if you are bold enough, even the laws of nature are with you.

Most everyone is familiar with Albert Einstein's Theory of Relativity. This theory is expressed in a simple formula: $E = mc^2$. That is to say, energy equals mass times the speed of light squared. This has become known as the theory of space and time. Space is defined as the three dimensions of matter: length, heighth, width. The fourth dimension, time, can be measured by the speed of light. The time dimension is dependent on the observer's motion and position in space. Einstein's theory is really two theories.

The Special Theory of Relativity states that: 1.) The speed of light in a vacuum is the same for all systems moving at constant velocity with respect to one another. 2.) Natural laws are, without exception, true for all systems moving at constant velocity with respect to one another.

The General Theory of Relativity states that: There exists a gravitional force whereby an object influences another with respect to time and place.

I'll not explore all the ramifications of what this means. Certainly I don't understand it that well, and I would only offend any of the scientific minds that may read this. The point I would like to make is that the actual operation of this theory works well when considering the vastness of the universe and the solar systems beyond ours. It seems to lose its practicability when viewed in the context of the experiences in my more local environment.

Our nearest galactic neighbor is the Andromeda Galaxy, a mere two million or so light-years away. In viewing the activities of our galactic neighbor, I can begin to apply the concept that we can look into the past of a faraway galaxy. The cause and effect attitude demonstrates to me the moving from the past to the present and on to predicting the future. I can begin to under-stand, in a limited manner, how the weak gravitational forces can actually bend the perception of time over these great distances.

The laws of physics, or natural laws, are there before us, avail-able for study and definition. Their definition does not take away from the evidence of the exisitence of the Supreme Being that was the original cause. In fact they cannot predict or describe it since God is outside of our space-time continuum. (See Gödel's Incompleteness Theorem for more on this.) Faith then becomes the link between our space-time continuum and God's. We can't ever know; we must believe.

Let me share with you my perception of the steps to scientific discovery.

Steps to Scientific Discovery

"Yet he has not left himself without testimony: He has shown kindness by giving you rain from heaven and crops in their seasons; he provides you with plenty of feed and fills your hearts with joy." (Acts 14:17)

Step	Reference	Text
Mystery	Job 11:7	Can you fathom the mysteries of God? Can you probe the limits of the Almighty?
Discovery	Deut. 29:29	The secret things belong to the Lord our God, but the things revealed belong to us and to our children forever, that we may follow all the words of this law.
Investigation	Proverbs 25:2	It is the glory of God to conceal a matter; to search out a matter is the glory of kings.
Definition	Psalms 19:2-4	Day after day they pour forth speech; night after night they display knowledge. There is no speech or language where their voice is not heard. Their voice goes out into all the earth, their words to the ends of the world.
Understanding	Romans 1:20	For since the creation of the world God's invisible qualities -- his eternal power and divine nature -- have been clearly seen, being understood from what has been made, so that men are without excuse.
Praise	Psalms 19:1	The heavens declare the glory of God; the skies proclaim the work of his hands.

The harmony of all of life is the result of the Creator. His natural laws are the borders within which we live our lives. My theory of relativity would be the definition of my relationship to my God. It is a natural law.

Milestone #3

Discover to the fullest that which is revealed to you.

1. Can you describe what you believe to be a natural law of science? Consider: what goes up must come down, for every action there is a reaction, opposites attract, etc.

2. Select two of the natural laws you have identified and discuss your perception of how these laws could have evolved over time. How did primitive man explain the happenings? What view would the ancient Egyptians or Assyrians have of the events? How would the philosophers of Greece explain them? What caused modern man to modify, or redefine, the natural laws?

3. Discuss the benefits in defining how things happen and the cause of the events.

4. Do you believe that investigation and understanding of the workings of nature strengthens or weakens one's faith in God? Explain your answer (Psalm 73:16-17).

5. Can pure scientists believe in a supreme being? Why, or why not?

6. How do the Steps to Scientific Discovery impact your relationship with God?

Quantum Mechanics

There are certain friends that we have had over the years that enjoyed getting involved in long and deep conversations of a philosophical nature. Once engaged in those conversations, they would last for hours and well into the early hours of the morning. During these discussions, we shared our ideals, discussed our beliefs, and searched for the meaning of life. There were only a very few friends that we would expose ourselves to in this manner. The discussions were never argumentive, but rather probing. Just trying to explain what one believes is sometimes difficult. I found that by explaining what I believed, sometimes what I thought I believed changed as I explained it.

At times we would get very animated in our explanations. We would draw concepts, or outlines, on paper and modify them as we discussed the thought. Looking back, I don't recall any great mystery that we uncovered, or any profound statement that we came to agreement on. But I do recall the interaction; the acknowledgement of what the other person thought, the extreme closeness we felt at the moment. It was not a time of scientific discovery, but it was a time of sharing.

Our children remember those long-night discussions and have often remarked how wonderful it was to be exposed to the openness of true friendship. While the specifics of those discussions have long since faded, the memory of the events live on. I particularly remember one all-night discussion with a bachelor friend of ours. Yvonne and the children had gone to bed hours before we stopped our discussion. Around six in the morning, my friend gave me a challenge. One that I could not turn down. He proposed that very few people could defend their Christian beliefs with strong logic. This friend was very intelligent and read books on just about every subject. He believed he could play the "devil's advocate" and cause most people to doubt their beliefs. At the time I was leading a group of eighth graders in Sunday School lessons.

I accepted my friend's challenge and told him that the eighth graders could defend their beliefs. So without preparation, and with only a couple of hours of sleep, my friend joined me at church. The only introduction that I gave to the group, was that our guest was there to ask some questions to gain insight on their faith. My friend did a good job in asking those probing, open-ended questions, and I facilitated the discussions. I was proud of the way the eighth graders responded. They did not falter and, in fact, asked questions in return. Following that session, my friend stated that he was impressed with the understanding those teenagers had of their beliefs.

A little side note I did not share with my friend is that the group had spent the last three months sharing with each other a study series titled, "Defending Your Faith". I will say that the group was very much enlightened by the discussion that day. They grew from the experience of sharing and spent the next couple of Sundays discussing how much more meaningful it was to talk with a non-Christian when you attempt to defend your beliefs. I didn't let them know my friend is indeed a Christian and was playing at being the devil's advocate.

The probing, questioning, sharing experiences bring understand-ing to oneself and sometimes to others. Questioning strengthens the faith of the faithful. Science does not diminish the glory of the Almighty. It brings understanding to the workings of the natural laws. It provides platforms for new growth in one's spirituality. I suspect that science will never really answer all the mysteries of what goes on around us.

Quantum mechanics is called the theory of matter. As the Theory of Relativity deals with the expanse of the far-reaching universes, the theory of matter relates to the natural laws concerning the smallest elements of matter. By understanding the composition and work-ings of the smallest elements, scientists propose that they can explain the workings of all things, big and small.

My understanding of the basic theorems supporting quantum mechanics are as follows:

1.) An event is not an event without an observer; 2.) The observer influences the observed; 3.) For each action in an event, all alternative actions are occurring simultaneously in another world, or dimension.

Statements such as these lead to some very intense thinking and discussion. Seemingly nonsensical questions take on new relevance. For example, does a tree falling in the forest make a sound if there is no one there to hear it? As investigation gets more sophisticated, quantum mechanics becomes the spring-board for many diverse findings and theories.

Matter is being defined to ever smaller elements. When I was in school, my learning never went beyond the electrons and protons of atoms. I might add that my lack of truly scientific motivation has not made it necessary for me to even question much beyond that. But now matter is defined with quarks as the smallest element, and the probability proposed that smaller elements, called strings, exist and even smaller elements than that may exist.

Forces impacting matter are also being further defined. There are the strong nuclear and electromagnetic forces; there are weak nuclear and gravitational forces. The weak gravitational force is incorporated in the General Theory of Relativity. Are there more forces to be discovered? Most likely there is as new methods are developed to measure cause and effect.

The Theory of Chaos has resulted in identifying fractals. From this scientists can find a pattern that is repeated time and time again in ever smaller, self-similar, versions. So from chaos comes order. Scientists are expanding their theories in many directions at the same time. Sometimes this seems to be taking divergent paths. There is the Theory of Probabilities and the Theory of Indeterminism. It leads to many areas of uncertainty in the scientific community.

Even this uncertainty can be grossly defined. In quantum mechanics it means that a particle, such as an electron, cannot have a well-defined position and a well-defined momentum at the same time. Therefore, it is impossible to say in advance what value will be obtained by a measurement. All that can be determined in advance are the probabilities. The very act of measuring will affect the value obtained. Into this is woven the process philosophy that asserts the primacy of becoming over being and stresses the openness and indetermination of nature. All this is to say that the future is not implicit in the present.

Scientists continue to delve deeper into the natural laws, gaining understanding and developing new theorems. Some scientists are questioning the Theory of Relativity and many of the theorums of quantum mechanics. In the end they are left with the explanation that all things are governed by natural laws and initial conditions. The initial conditions become the beginning point for the operation of the natural laws. No one has the answer to the cause of the initial conditions.

With all we know, and I propose with all we are to learn, we are left with certain mysteries. I am left with the lamentations of Job, "Can you fathom the mysteries of God? Can you probe the limits of the Almighty?" (Job 11:7)

The following table reflects some of the mysteries found in the Bible.

Six Great Mysteries

"Oh, the depth of the riches of the wisdom and knowledge of God! How unmeasurable his judgments, and his paths beyond tracing out!" (Ro. 11:33)

Category	Mystery	Validation
Determination	This is the plan for the whole world; this is the hand stretched out over all nations. For the Lord Almighty has purposed, and who can thwart him? (Isaiah 14:26-27)	From one man he made every nation of men, that they should inhabit he whole earth; and he determined the times set for them and the exact places where they should live. (Acts 17:26)
Selection	For he chose us in him before the creation of the world to be holy and blameless in his sight. In love he predestined us to be adopted as his sons through Jesus Christ, in accordance with his pleasure and will. (Ephessians 1:4-5)	For those God foreknew he also predestined to be conformed to the likeness of his Son, that he might be the firstborn among many brothers. And those he predestined, he also called; those he called, he also justified; those he justified, he also glorified. (Romans 8:29-30)
New Birth	The wind blows wherever it pleases. You hear its sound, but you cannot tell where it comes from or where it is going. So it is with everyone born of the Spirit. (John 3:8)	All these are the work of one and the same Spirit, and he gives them to each one, just as he determines. (1 Corinthians 12:11)
Prosperity of the Unchosen	You are always righteous, O Lord, when I bring a case before you. Yet I would speak with you about your justice: Why does the way of the wicked prosper? (Jer. 12:1)	Our fathers disciplined us for a little while as they thought best; but God disciplines us for our good, that we may share in his holiness. (Hebrews 12:10)
Future Life	Listen, I tell you a mystery: We will not all sleep, but we will all be changed--in a flash, in the twinkling of an eye, at the last trumpet. For the trumpet will sound, the dead will be raised imperishable, and we will be changed. (1 Corinthians 15:51-52)	Just as man is destined to die once, and after that to face judgment, so Christ was sacrificed once to take away the sins of the people; and he will appear a second time, not to bear sin, but to bring salvation to those who are waiting for him. (Hebrews 9:27-28)
Incarnation	Beyond all question, the mystery of godliness is great: He appeared in a body, was vindicated by the Spirit, was seen by angels, was preached among nations, was believed on in the world, was taken up in glory. (1 Timothy 3:16)	Then Simeon blessed them and said to Mary, his mother: 'This child is destined to cause the falling and rising of many in Israel, and to be a sign that will be spoken against. (Luke 2:34)

While geography separates me from my good friend and we do not have the opportunity for all night discussions on religion and philosophy, my sons and I continue the tradition. On a recent night, Bruce and I discussed quantum mechanics and its relationship with religious thought. On the notion of all alternative actions occurring in other worlds at the same time, Bruce asked if his alternative actions were being experienced by other physical beings that are an exact replica of himself. He went on to ask, "Does this mean that I, Bruce, am made up of many beings, or is each one of them a unique being?" This question was followed up with, "Is there a soul for each of the beings, or is there only one soul for all the possible alternatives to my being that will have an eternal exisitence?" My question in return was, "What being are you: the one I am experiencing before me now, one from the alternative actions, or the sum of them all?" As with many of these discussions, it concluded without answers. Only the questions remained. But in those questions, my beliefs take shape, my faith remains firm, my hope becomes stronger.

There are many that speak of contradictions in the Bible, in the teachings, in the faith. But one significant thing must be considered: God is not on the same level as man. There can be no contradictions in one level when comparing to another level. "No, we speak of God's secret wisdom, a wisdom that has been hidden and that God destined for our glory before time began." (I Corinthians 2:7)

The study of matter and the forces that control it cannot alter the role of God from the beginning of time, through the daily experiences, and into the end of time. "In his heart man plans his course, but the Lord determines his steps." (Proverbs 16:9)

Milestone #4

Accept that there are mysteries beyond
worldly understanding.

1. The last fifty years have brought more scientific discovery than all the other years of the existence of humans on this earth. Identify and discuss discoveries that have been both beneficial and detrimental to mankind and/or the environment, such as, the wheel, electrode tube, nuclear power.

2. Scientists state that all things are governed by natural laws and initial conditions. Do you believe that there will ever be a scientific explanation of initial conditions? Why, or why not? Does the "Big Bang Theory" explain the initial conditions of our universe, or does it just point to another initial condition? Discuss.

3. Is it conceivable that humans will eventually be able to define all there is to know about creation? About future life? Explain the impact on your faith to the answer given (Psalm 147:4-5).

4. Has there been an event in your life that you feel is mystical and unexplained? Describe the event and circumstances. Have others tried to convince you it was a non-spiritual phenomena? Can the search for rational explanation of events of this nature impact an individual's faith? How?

5. Is there a limit to understanding by humans? By God? Explain the difference.

6. Discuss the Six Great Mysteries identified in this chapter and their impact on your faith.

God

God Is

As our children were growing up, we were very specific in teaching them how to address the many people they came in contact with. In the very beginning we worked hard at getting "Ma-Ma" and Da-Da". This would later change to a more formal address, possibly as formal as Mother and Father. The children progressed from Ma-Ma to Mommy to Mom, and for me from Da-Da to Daddy to Dad or Pop. Mother and Father is only used by them when they speak of us in the third person. We're old fashioned and have never allowed them to call us by our first name.

In addressing others we were very careful in giving them the proper Mr., Mrs., Miss, Ms. (when it became an appropriate address), Aunt, Uncle, and the ever important Grandmother and Grandfather. As parents we were strict enforcers to these titles, even though Aunt and Uncle did not always mean direct family relationships.

As grandparents, however, the rules are different. The most important element is that we are not in the role of enforcer. Our grandson was trained much as his father was before him. It was interesting to see how our names would evolve in his vocabulary. Once Ryan was old enough to put syllables together, we were addressed as Granny-Mommy and Dit-Dad. Granny-Mommy has now changed to Gran-Mommy; I'm still Dit-Dad. Perhaps these names will continue to evolve. I'm grateful that he calls me. What he calls me is not as important as the fact that he wants to call and feels comfortable in calling. Whenever he calls me, Dit-Dad is like sweet music on the ears and it stirs the heart. Our first granddaughter now calls me Pop and it has the same affect.

Let me call your attention to the Book of Exodus, chapters 3 and 4. The scene is when Moses goes to the mountain and talks to

God at the burning bush. You will recall that Moses is not very confident of his ability to do the work that the Lord asks of him. I will recreate this scene for you and paraphrase the conversation. This is how I see the event:

> God tells Moses, "You are to lead my people out of Egypt." Moses responds, "OK Lord, lead your people out of Egypt...Excuse me Lord, but how am I going to do that?"
>
> God answers, "Go to the Pharaoh and tell him to let my people go." Moses then says, "OK Lord, I'll go tell the Pharaoh to let your people go...Excuse me Lord, but why will your people and the Pharaoh listen to me?"
>
> God says, "Tell them that I sent you to do so." Moses then responds with, "OK Lord, I'll tell them that You sent me...Excuse me Lord, just one more thing. Who do I say sent me?"
>
> God angrily states, "I am that I am! Tell them I AM sends you. Now get off your knees and go do my work."

I can certainly relate to Moses in that I often look for excuses as to why I can't do something. It is those times that I need a good, swift kick to set me in motion. The point I am making is that God says He is to be called I AM.

In years past I had read much of the Bible, some portions many times. But it has been only in recent years that I see it wasn't really sinking in. I recall being told by several people that, "Jesus was a good person, but the Bible doesn't claim that He is God. In fact, Jesus was silent on that subject in front of His accusers." Well, I just accepted that and said it really didn't matter. My more recent Bible readings have revealed to me how wrong I was. Yes, Jesus was silent before His accusers, but this was to fulfill the prophesies of Isaiah (53:7). The Gospel writer, John, has Jesus stating very boldly who He is. See the following table:

God is the Ultimate Truth
I believe a fundamental truth that "God is"

"God is" tells me of the unity of the agent (the Creator) and the action (His blessing) in all events. I see God's living presence in everything.

God is	Reference
God says, "I am who I am"	Exodus 3:14
Jesus says, "I am the Messiah"	John 4:25-26
"I am the bread of life"	John 6:35
"I am from above"	John 8:22
"I am the eternal one"	John 8:58
"I am the light of the world"	John 9:4-5
"I am the gate"	John 10:7-9
"I am the Son of God"	John 10:36
"I am the resurrection and the life"	John 11:25
"I am Lord and teacher"	John 13:13-15
"I am the way, the truth and the life"	John 14:6
"I am the true vine"	John 15:5
"I am the Alpha and the Omega"	Revelation 1:8

God, and His manifestation in the man Jesus, says, "I am"; therefore, God is. And Jesus is not claiming to be like God, or a God, but God! He is my Lord and Savior, my God!

After reading Jesus' words in the Gospel, it occurred to me that God is saying, "I AM ________!" He wants us to fill in the blank based on our need.

Are you hungry?   "I am the bread of life, the true vine."

Are you in darkness?   "I am the light."

Are you lost?   "I am the way."

Do you need understanding?   "I am teacher."

Are you searching for God?   "I am Messiah, Son of
                               God, Lord."

In Revelations (22:13) Jesus says, "I am the Alpha and the Omega, the First and the Last, the Beginning and the End." And I submit that He is also all that is between. Each of us can fill in the blank as Jesus says, "I AM." What is your need. Jesus can fulfill it. He is all I need. As Paul writes in his letter to the Philippians (4:19), "And my God will meet all your needs according to his glorious riches in Christ Jesus."

To speak of silence is to break that silence, and to speak of God is to end the pure identity of God for I cannot know the deity of God. I only know that He is the Ultimate Truth.

Milestone #5

See God's living presence in everything.

1. How much do you think God cares about what is happening in your life? On a scale of 1-10 (10 = high) rank the following and explain your ranking:

    ____ Personal conflict with your employer

    ____ Fellowship with family and friends

    ____ Parking space near the mall entrance

    ____ Your financial security

    ____ A head cold that has been hanging on for two weeks

    ____ Family members who do not yet know Christ

2. What other areas in your life do you wonder about God's care? Explain.

3. Read Psalm 145. What are the three attributes of God that you most appreciate? Give examples of how they are recognized in your life. What are the three most important attributes in verses 8, 13, 18? Why?

4. What has God done for you this week for which you are thankful?

5. Read Matthew 11:28-30. Share one current need or concern so that others in your group may pray for you.

6. Read Psalm 95:1-7. Worship God for who He is. Praise Him for all He means to you. Each person should present their own praise petition in a closing group prayer.

The Nature of God

When I have tried to describe home, I found myself using different definitions based on the situation. I have said that the home is the physical structure that is occupied by the family unit. Also, I have said that the home is a base of operations. Then at other times, I have defined it as a comfortable and relaxed environment offering security and happiness. Each of these descriptions apply.

As I thought about attempts to describe home, I realized that I actually acted differently depending on my attitude, at the moment, of what home was. In the physical structure of the household, I certainly acted out the role of the dutiful father and faithful husband. My attitude was one of determination to protect the family and provide for them. As a base of operation, I acted out the role of the worker bee. My attitude was one of enthusiasm, doing more and more for the sake of accomplishment. This home attitude was most prevalent at work. The physical structure of the home became an extension of the place of work. As an environment of comfort and relaxation, I acted out the role of the joyful man of leisure. My attitude was one of confidence as I willingly extended myself to others.

The changes in attitude occurred as I viewed home from the different natures that had formed in my mind. As my attitude changed, so did my actions. I moved from purposeful to visionary, from introvert to extrovert, from controlled to free-wheeling and back again.

An illustration of this is one that my dear wife, Yvonne, has reminded me of time and time again. When we had our place on the ocean, I would dash home from work, pack up the car, gather the family and head for the beach. The trip required driving over the Chesapeake Bay Bridge, cross the eastern shore of Maryland, cross the bridge over the back bay of Ocean City and finally pull into our parking place at the condominium. The 125-mile trip took little more than two hours, when not delayed by heavy traffic.

I could sense a change occurring in me as we got ever closer to our destination. Generally, I am a tense driver for it is a very responsible task. As we crossed the Bay Bridge, I could feel myself relaxing. I would turn on the radio or turn on a tape and sing along with the music. By the time I could smell the ocean water, I was completely relaxed and would be chattering away with Yvonne about the silliest of things. Yvonne didn't have to remind me that I was changing. I knew it, and I knew it wasn't any deliberate action on my part that caused it. Our time at the ocean was always a delight. But then for the trip home the reverse would happen. And it would begin about the time I started to pack up the car for the return trip.

More recently I reflected on this. I was the same person, yet I acted differently in each situation. The more I looked into this, I realized it wasn't the physical location that made the difference in my actions, but my attitude towards the environment. As I pulled together the three natures of home and my attitudes with them, I found the total person that I really am. There are negative attributes that tag along with the positive ones in each situation. I am still working with the effort of being the positive, total person all the time. It is difficult for me. Situations should not change my attitude. I must find the way to be the positive, caring self that I am capable of in all situations. But for now, I must use all the attributes I find in myself as I see them in the three natures of my home to describe who I am. The natures of my home, in effect, have resulted in the three natures I find in myself.

Whenever one begins to describe God, it seems to always begin by saying He is all-present (omnipresence), all-knowing (omniscience), and all-powerful (omnipotence). Indeed these are His attributes. By saying such, it gives some human measure to the capabilities of God. Some of the biblical references to these attributes are as follows:

Attributes of God

OMNIPRESENCE	
Acknowledge and take to heart this day that the Lord is God in heaven above and on the earth below. There is no other.	Deuteronomy 4:39
The eyes of the Lord are everywhere, keeping watch on the wicked and the good.	Proverbs 15:3
"Am I not a God nearby," declares the Lord, "and not a God far away? Can anyone hide in secret places so that I cannot see him?" declares the Lord. "Do not I fill heaven and earth?" declares the Lord.	Jeremiah 23:23-24
The Lord is near to all who call on him, to all who call on him in truth.	Psalm 145:18
OMNISCIENCE	
O Lord you have searched me and you know me. You know when I sit and when I rise; you perceive my thoughts from afar. You discern my going out and my lying down; you are familiar with all my ways. Before a word is on my tongue you know it completely, O Lord.	Psalm 139:1-4
Great is our Lord and mighty in power; his understanding has no limit.	Psalm 147:5
Do you not know? Have you not heard? The Lord is the everlasting God, the Creator of the ends of the earth. He will not grow tired or weary, and his understanding no one can fathom.	Isaiah 40:28
Nothing in all creation is hidden from God's sight. Everything is uncovered and laid bare before the eyes of him to whom we must give account.	Hebrews 4:13
OMNIPOTENCE	
I know you can do all things; no plan of yours can be thwarted.	Job 42:2
O Lord God Almighty, who is like you? You are mighty, O Lord, and your faithfulness surrounds you.	Psalm 89:8
The Lord does whatever please him, in the heavens and on the earth, in the seas and all their depths.	Psalm 135:6
Jesus looked at them and said, "With man this is impossible, but with God all things are possible."	Matthew 19:26

God's capabilities are beyond human understanding. To get to the nature of God though, you must move to another level. It is not enough to say that He is all-present, all-knowing, all-powerful. The essence of God is how these attributes are used. This then gets closer to explaining the unexplainable, the nature of God. He is the Total Being. He is the same in all situations. He is the positive force that influences every situation.

The Nature of God
Elements to the Truth

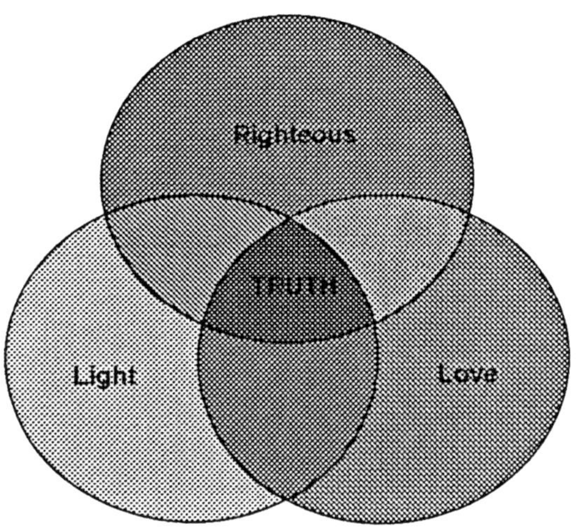

Previously, I have written that God is the Ultimate Truth. I see the Ultimate Truth occurring when all the elements of God's nature converge to a central core.

> **Light** — "This is the message we have heard from him and declare to you, God is light; in him there is no darkness at all." (1 John 1:5)

> **Righteous** — "If you know that he is righteous, you know that everyone who does what is right has been born of him." (1 John 2:29)

> **Love** — "God is love. Whoever lives in love lives in God, and God in him." (1 John 4:16)

Love comes from God. It is not only an element of the nature of God, but it is His very being.

Milestone #6

Know that the nature of God is the Ultimate Truth.

1. God's capabilities have often been defined as omnipresent, omniscience, and omnipotent. What do these attributes of God mean to you?

2. Read 1 John 1:5-7; it declares that God is light. What does it mean to walk in the light (John 3:19-21)?

3. Read 1 John 2:29; it declares that God is righteous. How would you define "being righteous"? Can a human being live a righteous life? What traits would someone have that lived what can best be defined as a righteous life? How does this compare with the traits that God may demonstrate as being righteous?

4. Read 1 John 4:7-5:5. Describe the difference, if any, between loving and being love. Are there different types of love? Discuss the Greek words for love: Agape, Phileon, Eros.

5. How would you define truth? Is being truthful in what you say the only demonstration of truth? Explain. If you perceive that a little girl is not pretty, and tell her so, is that truthful? Why, or why not?

6. How would you describe God? Can one fully describe, and understand, the nature of God? What, if any, are the limitations in any description of God?

The Holy Spirit

There is so much around us that goes unnoticed and is taken for granted. We travel life's journey without stopping "to smell the roses". Our lives are so filled with activities that we have little time to spend on any one event or on any one relationship. To me it seems that I too often operate in a reflex mode rather than taking the time and energy to understand the purpose of my actions and the impact of those actions on others. Like the Lone Ranger, I charged off to satisfy the impulse of the moment. But even the Lone Ranger took time to discuss his actions before-hand with his trusted companion, Tonto.

As our children were growing up, I can recall asking them on a number of occasions, "Why didn't you discuss this with me before you did that?" Now, I look back and wonder at the example I set for them. Certainly Yvonne and I discussed many things together before either of us took any action. But just as certain, there were many times when I didn't discuss important actions with Yvonne beforehand. On reflection, I see how much I needed the intuitive perspective she has. Maybe the action I ultimately took would not have changed, but I know I would have been better prepared for the resulting impact of my own actions. There was much I didn't notice before the action. How could I possibly have missed seeing what should have been so obvious?

I do not consider myself a good communicator. It is not uncommon for me to allow Yvonne to take the lead in carrying a conversation, whether it be between ourselves or with friends. The addition of a couple of granddaughters brought the realization that the female gender is particularly vocal. They talk, but they also want to be talked to. It was a lesson for me that was a long time in coming, but now recognized. I am striving to be more vocal with most everyone. Still, the natural tendency for me is to be silent.

From the time Sarah Anne was brought home from the hospital, I would carry her around the house and point to objects and tell her about those objects. I knew she didn't understand most of what I was telling her, but nonetheless, I would talk about the object and tell a story about some of them. I would say, "See!" and identify the item and go on to say whatever came to my mind about the item. Pictures, chairs, lamps, mirrors, flowers, pots, pillows all had a purpose as I tried to explain them to my granddaughter. As Sarah Anne got older, I took her outside in her stroller and walked through the neighborhood. Again, I would point to things and discuss them with her. Birds, animals, trees, flowers, houses, cars, people, mailboxes, shadows each had their own stories. I would mimic the sounds of birds and animals, and we would stop at anything that seemed to catch her interest.

On these excursions, both in the house and outside, she would point to whatever caught her interest. We would stop and I would talk about the object. When she heard enough, she would hold out her hand and repeatedly bring her fingers into the palm to indicate that it was time to move on. Somewhere along the way, I realized that she hadn't really noticed these objects until they were pointed out to her. Once she was made aware of them, she remembered and then enjoyed seeing them again and again. She began to mimic the sounds of the birds and animals. She began to jibber-jabber away as she took in the environment around her.

Now Sarah Anne points and says, "See!" She sees what she hadn't noticed before, and she wants to see more. See is such an important word to her, and has a very specific meaning to her. In showing her seagulls, her response is now, "See! Gulls!" There is so much more for her to see. There is so much more I want to show her. I have shown her many things, but now she shows me things I have not noticed before. As I had a hand in opening her eyes, she now is opening my eyes. The teacher has become the pupil. The wonderful thing about this is that we are seeing together.

Likewise, we are not left alone to find our way to God. He sent us the Holy Spirit to guide us, instruct us, interpret the Word for us, intercede for us. The Spirit brings us the calling and stays with us until sainthood. Indeed this is a precious gift from God. "If you then, though you are evil, know how to give good gifts to your children, how much more will the Father in heaven give the Holy Spirit to those who ask him!" (Luke 11:13)

Once we ask for the Holy Spirit, and have received it through baptism, it dwells within us to lead us every step of our journey here on earth. "Don't you know that you yourselves are God's temple and that God's Spirit lives in you?" (1 Corinthians 3:16)

The Old Testament tells us of how the Spirit came with power in those special times of need: to Othniel (Judges 3:10), Gideon (Judges 6:34), Samson (Judges 14:6), Saul (1 Samuel 10:10), David (1 Samuel 16:13); to bring understanding to the 70 elders with Moses (Numbers 11:25). How fortunate we are that the Spirit is with us each and every day. The following table reflects how the Spirit works with us and nurtures our spiritual growth from the sinner, to believer to sainthood.

Workings of the Holy Spirit

"...the Spirit helps us in our weaknesses." (Romans 8:26)

in the Sinner		in the Believer		in the Saint	
Workings	Text	Workings	Text	Workings	Text
The Call	Joel 2:18	Conversion	Ro 8:16	Justification	1 Co 6:11
The Law Contrition	2 Pe 1:21	Repentance	Ac 2:38	Sanctification	1 Pe 1:2
Guide Awakening Illumination Persuasion	Jn 16:13	Inner Trans- formation	Ro 8:9	Union with God	Eph 4:13
The Gospel Faith	Jn 14:26	Regeneration	Ro 8:11	Eternal Peace	Rev 22:17

The Holy Spirit has a special gift for each of us. As Paul explains (Galations 5:23-24), "But the fruit of the Spirit is love, joy, peace, patience, kindness, goodness, faithfulness, gentleness and self-control. Against such things there is no law."

Milestone #7

Receive the gift of the Holy Spirit.

1. What is the source of the Holy Spirit (Isaiah 11:2, 42:1; Matthew 3:16)? When did you receive the Holy Spirit, or was it received for you by someone else? Explain.

2. A gift may be offered, but it is not really a gift until it is accepted by the receiver. Can the Holy Spirit be considered a gift (Luke 11:13)? Once accepted, is the Holy Spirit always with us (1 Corinthians 6:19)?

3. Discuss the apparent progression of the fullness of the indwelling spirit represented in the graphic, Working of the Holy Spirit.

4. How did Jesus describe the Holy Spirit (John 14:15-17)? What does that mean to you personally?

5. Do you feel the Holy Spirit has been active in your life? How? Have you ever felt spiritually empty? What did you do, or should you do, to achieve a fullness of the Holy Spirit?

6. What is the result of living a spirit filled life (Galations 5:23-24)? Discuss what that means to you.

The Trinity

The year was 1924. The location was a rural community in northwestern Georgia. A man and his family were going on a brief automobile trip to town. The father and mother climbed into the car with their youngest child. A young twelve year old son was told to stay home with a younger brother and work at cutting corn stalks in the field. The father's twin sister and her husband were going into to town with them and there wasn't enough room in the car for all of them. The young boy reluctantly stayed behind and didn't even say good bye to his parents as they prepared for their ride to town. It was a journey that had been taken many times before, but it was a journey that would not be taken again in the same manner.

The father's car headed off and the young son watched from the field. He longed to be with his parents, even for this brief trip, because he really enjoyed the closeness he had with his parents. But he had been given work responsibility for himself and his brother. Besides the trip wouldn't be too long. He could not imagine how long it would really become.

Down the road a bit, at a place called Crown Mill Crossing, the father's car stalled. From out of nowhere a train appeared. The car was stalled on the tracks. Then there was the crashing sounds of the train plunging into the side of the car. A father, a mother, a young brother, an aunt, an uncle and a family friend were all dead. It was so sudden, so sad, so tragic. Three thousand friends and neighbors attended the funeral service to express their sympathy and show compassions for the family. It was a memory that would forever haunt the young boy. A lingering guilt about the angry thoughts of not being able to go to town remained, as did the sadness of not having said a last good-bye.

My father's life changed from that moment on. The mis-handling of the family's estate and the placing of the surviving children in boarding schools were decisions that this boy would

have no voice in. But he would be able to make his own decisions in time.

Dad was quite a scholar. He intended to complete college and
become a history teacher. But instead, he quit college six
months before completing his senior year and never went back to
obtain his degree. His life took many turns. He was a cowboy,
he operated a still and his restless adventure eventually took him
to the sea. He worked as a deck hand. To my good fortune, it
was in this adventure that he met the pretty young woman that
would become my mother.

Through the years I got bits and pieces of his life story. But he
guarded his comments and was never too open about any of it.
Particularly, he never discussed the fatal accident that changed
his life or the impact of the haunting memories. I look back on
fragmented stories and hold them all dear to me. Those stories
would make quite a "stranger than fiction" novel.

When we moved out of the center city to a suburb, I visited a
local park and saw tennis courts for the first time. I told Dad that
I would like to try the game. He dug through the closet and
pulled out an old tennis racket. It had a medal frame and wire
string webbing. At ten years old, it was all I could do just to
hold it. We talked about tennis and Dad shared stories of his
victories when in college. He never said he wanted to play
again, but the game must have meant something special for him
to keep the racket for those years. Then there was the baseball
glove. I was in my early teens when Dad let me use the glove. It
was barely more than a couple of pieces of leather laced together.
One really had the sense of catching a ball with that glove.
These are cherished keepsakes.

Neither my father nor I are very talkative. But when we did get
into discussions, I always listened intently for his insight. He
had a down-home type of philosophy that appealed to me. He
also had a remarkable memory. It seemed he never forgot

anything he heard or read. One of the things that impressed me
most was his knowledge of the Civil War. I remember him
telling me on more than one occasion that a particular text book
was wrong on the facts of the Civil War. Research into the
subject proved my Dad was right.

What I remember most about my father was his love and devotion to my Mother and to his two children. He was a dedicated
provider, a tireless worker and a caring father. I could not have
asked for a better role model.

I look back and see the restless adventurer, the gifted teacher, the
wonderful father. All these were within him at all times. Three
persons in one. Each very much unique to the other. Each
would be enough to make a person complete on its own. But
together the three made a person bigger than life itself.

The Trinity is one of the mysteries of the Bible that cannot
possibly be explained or really understood in human terms.
Often, when asked to explain this, I have used the comparison
that I am three persons in one. To my father, I am son; to my
son, I am father; to my wife, I am spouse. This example comes
woefully short of giving any understanding to the Holy Trinity.

I have heard theologians express it by saying that water has three
forms: solid, liquid and gas. Depending on the circumstance,
water comes in the form appropriate for the environment. While
I can understand the conditions under which water changes form,
I still have a difficult time with the mystery of the Trinity.

It is interesting to note that only once in the Old Testament is
Holy used three times in one phrase. The prophet Isaiah (6:3)
announces the trinity, "Holy, Holy, Holy." The term "fullness"
occurs only three times in the Bible:

      Ephesians 3:19   "the fullness of God (the
                                        Father)"

Ephesians 4:13   "the fullness of Christ (the
                        Son)"

Colossians 2:9   "the fullness of the Godhead
                        (the Holy Spirit)"

Matthew (3:16-17) reports the trinity: "As soon as Jesus was
baptized, he went up out of the water. At that very moment
heaven was opened, and he saw the Spirit of God descending
like a dove and lighting on him. And a voice from heaven said,
'This is my Son, whom I love, with him I am well pleased.'"

RELATIONSHIP OF THE THREE PERSONS IN ONE
ONE GOD = THREE MANIFESTATIONS

God the Father	Jesus the Son	the Holy Spirit
The Creator Genesis 1:1	Exact Representation John 14:9 Hebrews 1:3	The Regenerator Romans 8:13
The Source of Life	The Way John 14:6	The Comforter John 14:16-17
The Creative Thought	The Word John 1:1, 14 1 John 1:1	The Activator Ezekiel 36:27 John 16:13
Elohim = God Genesis 1:1	YAHWEH = Lord Genesis 3:23	Ruach = Spirit Genesis 6:3

The Activator activates the creative Word and relates it to that which is created. Our Creator speaks to us through Jesus and we hear through the Holy Spirit. "To God's elect...who have been chosen according to the foreknowledge of God the Father, through the sanctifying work of the Spirit, for obedience to Jesus Christ and sprinkling of His blood." (1 Peter 1:2)

As I reflect on the being of man, I understand that we are made of mind, body and soul. This comes closer to giving me some understanding. The workings of the mind is a complete mystery to me. Science can explain how it is formed and how electrical impulses are transmitted along the nervous system. But still they cannot adequately explain how the mind really works. The creation of thought, the storing of memory, the training of capabilities and the development of intuitive responses are all the result of unseen forces at work. This to me represents God the Father. The physical body is well explained, certainly beyond my understanding. It is easy for me to relate to the touchy-feely experience of the physical being. This to me represents Christ the Son. Documentation of Jesus' earthly existence and His teachings are evidence enough for me. Just as I have a relative understanding of the physical body, so do I have a relative understanding of the Son. The soul, or spirit, then represents the Holy Spirit to me. Again, I am without understanding of how it works, but I have the awareness of it's presence.

Three-in-one I understand. But a full understanding of any of the components is not within me. I am left with a mystery of my very being which I see as a little trinity. How much greater a mystery is the Holy Trinity!

THE TRINITY
God's Relationship to Mankind

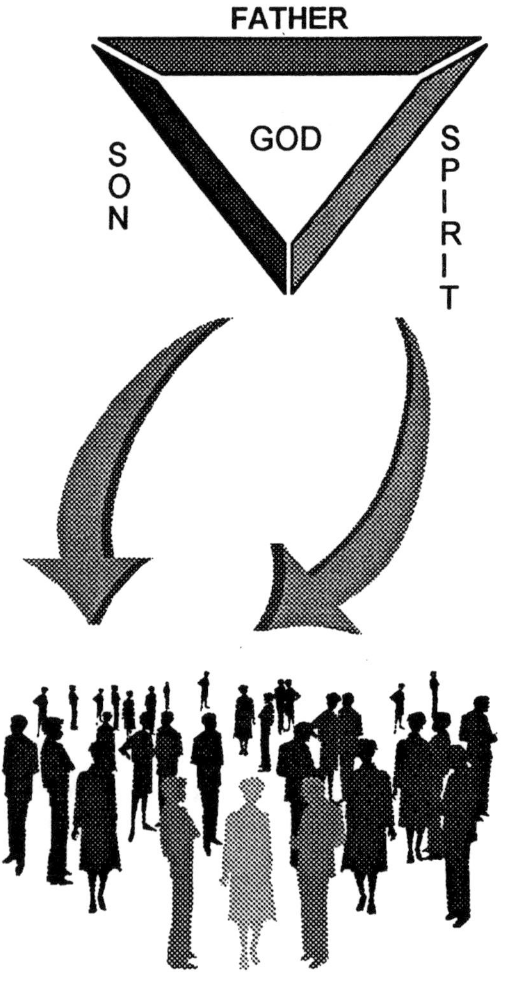

God has reached down to mankind through the sacrifice of His Son and the gift of the Holy Spirit. Mankind has a responsibility to respond. To receive the fellowship of God, mankind has to reach out and accept the gift.

Milestone #8

Accept the mystery of the Trinity.

1. How would you explain the term Creator as it applies to God? What has God created? If a child is born through the actions of a man and woman, what role, if any, does God the Creator play?

2. Read John 1:1. In Greek the term "word" is expressed as rhema or logus. Rhema is interpreted to mean " an utterance". Logus is the root word for logic, or rationalization. The latter term is used in John 1:1. What does the term "word" mean to you in this verse? Is it more than the spoken or written word of our language? Explain.

3. Read Romans 8:12-15. How does the Holy Spirit help us to regenerate spiritual growth? What does the concept of sonship mean to you?

4. Describe, in your own words, the meaning to the three-persons-in-one as declared in the Holy Trinity?

5. Explain the relationship of the Holy Trinity to mankind.

6. Do you feel that you understand the Trinity? What questions, if any, remain unanswered? If there are still unanswered questions, can you accept belief of, and faith in, the Trinity? Why, or why not?

Spiritual Unity

As I think about unity, I relate to the family unit. The husband and father in the typical role of the cornerstone of the family. The wife and mother as the binding force, or keystone, of that family. The children are the building blocks of the family. When all these components are in harmony, the family is a powerful force, a force that can overcome any obstacle.

Our family has been blessed in that we have always been close and have been quick to respond to the needs of each other. This closeness can easily be taken for granted. It may not even be in the everyday awareness of the family members. But in those times of trial and tribulation, that closeness becomes the family force to make right the situation.

About seventeen years ago, I decided that I should have my own business. After all, I had been successful in my career with a large Fortune 50 conglomerate and a modest-sized consumer services firm. I had demonstrated an ability to guide big and small organizations to higher levels of achievement. The self-talk from my ego (pride) told me that I could do anything I set my mind to. Call it a mid-life crisis, a change of life, a search for identity, or something such as that, but I had a desire to do this wonderful thing on my own.

With very little capital and only a general concept of what I was going to do, I started a management consulting firm. I was so naive that I didn't realize that most business executives considered management consultants as unemployed individuals that couldn't make it in the real world of business. I was so confident of my own success that I went out and rented an office large enough for several people, purchased office furnishings, and even purchased one of those new mini-computers (this was several years before the introduction of the personal computer).

What a surprise to find out that people were not standing in line waiting for the wonderful things I could do for them. The realization that my family was depending on me to provide their support suddenly hit me. I was having a grand time visiting with business executives, discussing ways I could help them, writing and submitting proposals, but I wasn't generating any income. It was time to get serious with this game. I set myself in motion, and began getting some business. Then another problem became evident. Getting the business required me doing the work. If I did the work, I wasn't able to bring in more business. If I didn't bring in more business, the income would stop. I was literally running in circles. There was no such thing as a workday. Sometimes I would work 36 hours straight without stopping. There were no weekends or holidays or vacations.

Without even asking, the family stepped in. Yvonne took over the responsibility of running the office. Bruce had a full-time job elsewhere, but worked nights and weekends to perform required tasks to fulfill contracts. Michael was preparing to enter the Naval Academy and he also worked in the office and made our deliveries. Even Stephanie, who was in junior high school, did administrative duties and general typing. Slowly, the business stabilized and I was able to bring in additional salaried help. The business flourished. My dear wife continued to be involved as long as we had the business. Family force saved the business and saved the unity of the family.

The energy and force that comes from an experience like this is somewhat unimaginable. It reinforces that bonding of the family. The force itself becomes an ever-increasing force. My love and respect for my family grew during those years. Not because of the work they did, but because of the love for me and each other that became action and the care they demonstrated. Yvonne not only was the binding for the family, but also for the business. She took on those responsibilities without complaint or bitterness. It was during this period of time that we became the best of friends. Our total family was involved, taking on tasks, putting aside self-pleasures. The unselfish giving, the sharing, the loving and the caring was an overwhelming, willing, family communion. That work effort did not make us a unified family, but it did reflect the completeness, the wholeness, of family unity. The strength of each family member intensified the strength of the complete family and nurtured the growth of all.

There is a completeness in God that nurtures our spiritual growth. We are all of His family. It is His desire that we have the fullness of that family fellowship. Experiencing this fellowship brings us peace and joy, even though we are at times called upon to work at achieving that experience. When God's work is at hand, we can go forward, willingly and with confidence, in union with God.

There is a unity in our very being and the being of God. Paul, in his letter to the Ephesians (4:3-6), states it this way, "Make every effort to keep the unity of the Spirit through the bond of peace. There is one body and one Spirit — just as you were called to one hope when you were called — one Lord, one faith, one baptism, one God and Father of all, who is over all and through all and in all."

As Paul describes it, I visualize an arch, or doorway, which invites us all to enter. This can be graphically shown as follows:

7 Elements of Spiritual Unity

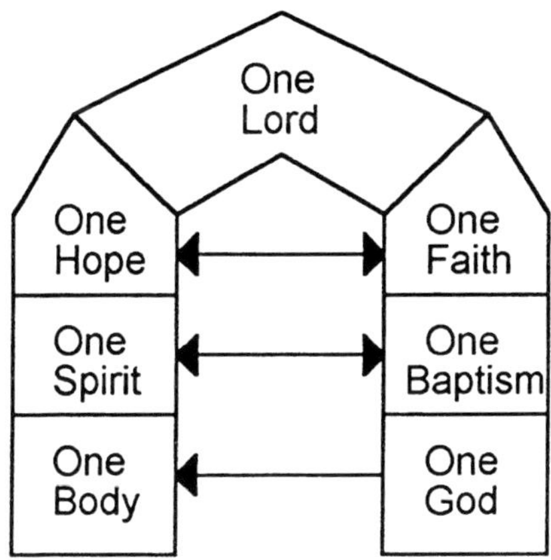

Body — We are all members of one body, the church (Romans 12:5).

Spirit — There is one Spirit is within us that guides us (John 16:13-15).

Hope — There is but one hope (Romans 8:24, 15:4).

Lord — Jesus is the keystone of our spiritual unity (Ephesians 1:23).

Faith — Faith is a requirement for salvation (Romans 10:17, Hebrews 11:1, 1 John 5:4). Without faith there is no hope and vice versa (Colossians 1:5, 1 Corinthians 13:13). Our hope is in our faith in Jesus.

Baptism — Baptism with water is a sign of purification (Mark 16:16, John 3:5, Acts 22:16). This was a practice before Christ (Ezekiel 36:25, see also Leviticus and Numbers). Christ has baptized us in the Spirit (Matthew 3:11, Mark 1:6, Luke 3:16).

God — At the cornerstone is the Father, one God of all members of the body (Exodus 20:3, Deuteronomy 6:4).

Milestone #9

Experience the completeness of spiritual unity.

1. There has been much recently written about the decline of the nuclear family. Discuss the present status of the family unit. How has it changed over the past 100 years? What are the barriers to maintaining the family as a complete unit?

2. What impact has the change in the family unit had on our society? On our nation? Do you feel it is different in other parts of the world? If so, how?

3. What are the enablers for building a strong family unit? How would you describe the ideal family unit?

4. Has a family member ever done something that you did not like, or you were very opposed to in principle? How did it make you feel? How did you react to the situation? Did you experience some distance in the closeness you once had for each other? Did this impact your fellowship with the family member? Does that mean a change in relationship?

5. In your own words, describe the elements of spiritual unity. How do each of these elements promote spiritual growth?

6. How does a family unit as described in 3. above compare to the Kingdom of God?

Jesus

Prophecies

It wasn't long after Bruce was born that Yvonne said he and I would work together. This was a statement that she repeated many times over the years. Perhaps this foretelling had something to do with my desire to start my own business and provide a place for my children to work and express themselves. This may or may not have been one of the driving forces for going out on my own, but I certainly liked the idea of being with all my children each and every day. A family business would provide that opportunity. But what business would appeal to us all? My career was directed toward financial and general management. Bruce's interest grew in the scientific and technical areas.

At any rate, I began a business as discussed in a previous chapter. Bruce went on his way with a degree in higher mathematics and a technical background that was beyond my understanding. Bruce talked little about his career, but we sensed that his career was on a roller-coaster ride similar to the one I was on. Then several years ago, Bruce made another job change and it was obvious that things were becoming much more stable for him. At that time, I was struggling with a one-person business that had its peaks and valleys of success. When business was good, I brought in sub-contractors to perform many of the required tasks. The good cycles were losing their frequency, but I was determined to make a moderate success of the business.

Then one April evening I received a call from Bruce asking if I would be interested in helping him out on an engagement in Rochester, New York. He said it was only a three-month effort, but he needed someone with a strong business background and an understanding of project management concepts. I told him I would be interested and he got the necessary approval from his California employer. Well, Bruce and I were now working together again except I was reporting to him. It wasn't what I had envisioned twenty years before.

The three-month engagement extended to two years. During the second year, Bruce's employer made repeated efforts to have me join their firm on a full-time basis. I resisted, because I still had this dream to make my business successful and provide a working place for my children. One day I realized that this dream I wouldn't let go of was rooted in self-pride and independence. Wasn't it just a year or so ago I vowed to Christ that I was turning my life over to Him and was willing to let go of everything? I was holding back. Needless to say, I prayed about the situation and asked Yvonne to participate in the prayer requests and decision. I joined the company as a full-time employee. Bruce and I are still working together.

I have found much satisfaction in working with Bruce. It gave me an opportunity to be with him frequently, not only in the work environment but also in the more casual environment of spending evenings together in various out-of-town locations. It was time I would not have had otherwise. I learned much from the experience: including a clearer understanding of myself and a fuller understanding of Bruce.

Through the years I have always been proud of him. He excelled in school and sports. He graduated from Johns Hopkins. He was a good person in that he was honest, sincere and caring. There wasn't anything he wouldn't do for the family. But on to that I added an understanding of how wonderfully qualified he is in the work he does. I always knew he was a quick learner, but now I witnessed how he put his technical expertise to practical application. His caring extended beyond the family to the interests of the clients. Now I seek out his counsel for the assignments I have at work. Roles have changed. My son is a respected peer. He has grown, but I have grown all the more because of working with him. As a team we accomplish much for the benefit of our clients, for the benefit of our employer, for the greater bonding of our own relationship. I cherish the time we are together.

Yvonne did prophesy our working relationship. My selfish desires may have mis-interpreted the real meaning. Was it just a hopeful desire? Possibly so, but isn't that a meaningful aspect to many prophecies.

There are more than three hundred prophecies in the Old Testament concerning the life and death of Jesus Christ. Details of the birth, life, death and resurrection of Jesus, along with the purpose of His coming to earth, were foretold by prophets that preceded Him by 200 to 1500 years. The New Testament records the fulfillment of these prophecies and often refers to the Old Testament text.

Only a few of the prophecies have been shown in the following table to reflect the level of detail in the prophecies. While there may be multiple references for any one of the prophecies, only a single reference is recorded for each prophecy and its corresponding fulfillment. Again, this is not intended to be a full study on the subject, but rather a quick reference to support the concept.

THE TRUTH REVEALED

"Then the Lord replied, 'Write down the revelation and make it plain on tablets so that a herald may run with it. For the revelation awaits an appointed time; it speaks of the end and will not prove false. Though it linger, wait for it; it will certainly come and will not delay.'" (Habakkuk 2:2-3)

Subject	Prophecy	Fulfillment
Offspring of a woman	Genesis 3:15	Luke 2:7
Virgin birth	Isaiah 7:14	Matthew 1:18-23
Birthplace in Bethlehem	Micah 5:2	Luke 2:4-7
Childhood in Egypt	Hosea 11:1	Matthew 2:14-15
Ministry in Galilee	Isaiah 9:1-2	Matthew 4:12-16
Triumphant entry	Zechariah 9:9	John 12:12-14
His betrayal	Psalm 41:9	Mark 14:43-45
30 pieces of silver	Zechariah 11:12-13	Matthew 27:3-10
Scourged and spit upon	Isaiah 50:6	Matthew 26:67
His crucifixion	Psalm 22	Matthew 27
Given gall and vinegar	Psalm 69:21	John 19:29
Purpose of His death	Isaiah 53:4-6	1 Peter 2:24
His resurrection	Psalm 16:9-10	Luke 24:1-12
His ascension	Psalm 68:18	Luke 24:50-51

As Jesus taught, He relied much on the Old Testament to reinforce the will of God and give insightful meaning to the inspired words of God.

Additionally, the life and works of prominent Old Testament personalities can be seen as being repeated in Jesus. Adam, Abraham, Isaac, Jacob, Joseph and Moses have all been compared to Jesus. What they individually, symbolically accomplished for their people has been fulfilled for all people in Jesus. What was accomplished in part by the high priest Melchizedek and the important prophets, such as Elijah and Elisha, has been made complete in Jesus. Even the ritualistic observance of God by the Israelites and the symbolism of their temple were a foretelling of God's plan for salvation. But these comparisons will be left for another journey.

Milestone #10

Recognize the prophecies of Jesus have been fulfilled.

1. Did you ever feel that you sense something was going to happen? How did this premonition come to you (in a dream, an uneasy feeling, sudden thought, hope, etc.)? Did the event actually occur? If so, was it as anticipated? Why was it so important?

2. Do you believe that certain individuals have an ability to actually predict future events? If so, what is the source of the phenomena? Is it a skill or sensitivity that can be developed?

3. The Old Testament identifies many prophets that appeared in a succeeding chain that spanned centuries. What was the role that these prophets played in the history of the Hebrew nation? Do you feel that they were directed by God? How?

4. Do you feel that these prophets foretold future events that actually happened?   Do you believe the prophecies concerning the Hebrew nation were actually written, or spoken, by these prophets, or rather were they a matter of reconstruction history?

5. There are more than 300 prophecies concerning the Messiah in the Old Testament. Do you feel the prophecies identified as pertaining to Jesus actually apply to Him? Do you consider them general in nature, or were they specific revelation? How do you justify your position?

6. What do you believe Jesus means when He says that He has come to fulfill the Law and the Prophets (Matthew 5:17)? Do you feel Jesus has, in fact, fulfilled the prophecies? On what do you base your feelings in this matter?

The Nature of Jesus

November 23, 1991 was a day that I had anxiously awaited for some time. I had flown into Charleston the night before and Cheryl and Ryan were now taking me to the Navy Yard to board a Navy tug for the next step of my journey. As I stood on the steel deck at the stern of the tug, I looked out to Cheryl and Ryan and quietly gave thanks for being blessed with such a wonderful daughter-in-law and grandson. Then I remembered I had my newly acquired camcorder with me and I began to test out the operations of the 10:1 zoom lens. The tug jolted as the two large propellers started churning the waters. Slowly we pulled away from the dock and Cheryl and Ryan drifted into the background. Even with the zoom lens they were only visible for a few minutes. The tug picked up speed as it passed the Navy Shipyard. The battery of Old Charleston came and passed so quickly. Then Fort Sumpter appeared on the horizon before us and slowly drifted by, then passed into the distance. For more than an hour the tug sped out of the still waters of the Charleston harbor heading for the Atlantic Ocean.

As we slowly circled at the designated waiting area, I trained my camcorder viewer out toward the ocean, moving slowly from side to side and zooming in and out. Then I saw it. A small speck coming out of the mist, looming ever larger as it approached the expectant tug. It was an awesome sight, the USS TECUMSEH, a nuclear powered ballistic missile submarine. The tug maneuvered closer and the size of the submarine dwarfed the appearance of the large tug. I tried capturing all the activities of the two large ships meeting, but I was more intent on locating a specific individual. Then I got him in focus. He was impressive in how he held himself and gave commands to the scurrying seamen. This was Lieutenant Commander R. Michael Johnson, Weapons Officer, my son. Emotions of pride and joy filled my very being. Hastily I jumped aboard the sub with great anticipation for I was about to spend three days with my son in his work environment. A got a little wave of acknowledgment from Michael when boarding. The warmer greeting and hug would come later after the sub was secure and headed back to sea.

A few pages can not possibly describe the impressions, observations and understanding that I obtained in my adventure aboard the TECUMSEH. Each passing moment gave me new insight to my son. The already puffed-up pride in Michael grew as I witnessed how he conducted himself in action and how much everyone on board respected him. Before this Michael was the son that I had to take care of and be concerned about. Certainly, he had grown into an independent young man, but I couldn't let go of that image of a son and the element of his nature that was really an extension of myself.

Now there is another nature to Michael that I had never internalized before — Michael at work. This indeed was a different Michael. A person that acted with formality and a leader of many, someone intent on the job before him and atuned to the many influences impacting his many decisions. This is not to say he was an entirely different person, for he was the same. The attributes of a fine son also made him a fine leader. Qualities of truth, sincerity, dedication and a sense of fairness were evident. These indeed were the building blocks for the traits of decisiveness, justice and hard work that made him a fine commander.

I certainly enjoyed his personal, guided tour of the sub and his knowledgeable explanation of the workings within. I was thrilled to be with him in command and share meals with him in the officers mess. I was elated at the successful completion of the war games played as we cruised hundreds of feet below the waters surface. Then I remember the time we spent together on the bridge. I felt closer to Michael than I had ever felt before, and at the same time I felt closer to God. A misty rain came from the clouds that veiled the majesty of the moon and stars, yet we sensed their presence. That cool, dark night brought a solemn reverence to the scene. The sound of the waves, the endless expanse of the water, the darkness reminding us of the unknown before us, all spoke of the presence of God and His direction of the destiny of those on board the TECUMSEH.

Too quickly the three days passed and we were docking at Port Canaveral, Florida. As I left to make my airplane connection for the trip home, I looked back to the large, dark monster that was my home for a brief period of time. I was reminded of a passage, "How many are your works, O Lord! In wisdom you made them all; the earth is full of your creatures. There is the sea, vast and spacious, teeming with creatures beyond number — living things both large and small. There the ships go to and fro, and the leviathan, which you formed to frolic there." (Psalm 104: 24-26)

How much the TECUMSEH would have seemed to be that mythical monster, the leviathan, to our forefathers. Indeed we did frolic, not with any evil intent, but on the side of righteousness.

The impressions that now are most strongly on my mind are those of Michael and how I have now seen his two natures. One at home, as the loving, caring and supportive son. The other on his turf, at work, as the strong-willed, just and respected leader. Two different people? Certainly not. Two different natures. No, not really. The elements of a good son and those of a good leader are always present. They all make up the true nature of Michael. I know Michael better; I understand him more; I grew up some in the experience.

The essence of the Christian faith, the thing that sets Christians apart, is the acknowledgment of the nature of Jesus. He was certainly the supportive Son, and He is the respected leader of the Christian faith. Simply stated, Jesus was totally human and is totally divine.

There are those that acknowledge His humanness and say that He was a good person, a great teacher, a wise prophet, but they do not accept Him as God. There are others that acknowledge His deity and say that He came down from heaven and visited earth in a divine state, in the appearance of a human, but they do not accept Him as human. Both groups have much more to learn about Jesus. It is necessary to understand the total being of Jesus to derive the impact on one's life that His presence can bring. The greater the understanding of the nature of Jesus, the more confidence one has in their faith as a Christian.

It is of utmost importance to me to acknowledge both the human and deity nature of Jesus. In His humanness, I can relate to the mission He had here on earth. I can relate to His disappointments and sufferings. I can relate to His very practical teachings. In His deity, I can approach God with confidence for I know that He, Jesus, understands the trials and tribulations I face. I hold Him in reverence for the position He holds at the right hand of the Father. I know that He has gone to prepare a place for me. The more I learn about Jesus, the more I grow in spirituality.

The evidence of the nature of Jesus is extensive, both in the Bible and the writings outside of the Bible. Following is a brief compilation of the biblical evidence:

Elements of the Nature of Jesus

"For to us a child is born, to us a son is given, and the government will be on his shoulders, and he will be called Wonderful Counselor, Mighty God, Everlasting Father, Prince of Peace." (Isaiah 9:6)

Element	Reference	Text

Humanity of Jesus:

Element	Reference	Text
His suffering as man	Genesis 3:15	And I will put enmity between you and the woman, and between your offspring and hers; he will crush your head, and you will strike his heal.
His human birth	Galations 4:4	But when the time had fully come, God sent his Son, born of a woman, born under the law
His natural growth	Luke 2:40	And the child grew and became strong; he was filled with wisdom, and the grace of God was upon him.
He was tempted and hungered	Luke 4:2	where for forty days he was tempted by the devil. He ate nothing those days, and at the end of them he was hungry.
He was tired and thirsty	John 4:6	Jacob's well was there, and Jesus, tired as he was from the journey sat down by the well.
He slept	Luke 8:23	As they sailed, he fell asleep.
He showed emotions	Matthew 26:37	He took Peter and two sons of Zebedee along with him, and he began to be sorrowful and troubled.

Deity of Jesus:

Element	Reference	Text
His name	Matthew 1:23	"The virgin will be with child and will give birth to a son, and they will call him Immanuel"-- which means, "God with us."
Son of God, the Father	John 5:17	Jesus said to them, "My Father is always at his work to this very day, and I, too, an working."
Equal with God	John 10:30	I and the Father are one.
Teaches with authority	Matthew 7:29	because he taught as one who had authority, and not as their teachers of the law.
Controls nature	Matthew 8:27	The men were amazed an asked, "What kind of man is this? Even the winds and the waves obey him."
Overpowers evil	Mark 1:27	The people were so amazed that they asked each other, "What is this? A new teaching-- and with authority! He even gives orders to evil spirits and they obey him."
Reigns over all things	John 3:35	The Father loves the Son and has placed everything in his hands.

Milestone #11

Believe in both the humanity and deity of Jesus.

1. Who is the person you most admire? What are the character-
    istics of that person that make him/her so admirable?

2. What additional characteristics would you add to this list to
    define the ideal person?

3. From what you have read and heard about Jesus, what traits
    reflect His human nature? Compare each of those traits to
    your ideal person. Do you have those same traits, in some
    measure? What traits do you not have? Could you have
    them? If not, why not?

4. What are the elements that reflect a divine nature to Jesus?
    Do any of these elements, or traits, exist in any person you
    know? Do you feel they ever could be obtained by any
    human?

5. Some people have claimed that Jesus is a God that placed
    Himself on earth for a brief period of time to do good works;
    others have claimed that He was just some type of godly
    manifestation that really only appeared to be in human form;
    and still others have claimed He was just a good person who
    lived a righteous life and was a charismatic teacher. Do any
    of these descriptions satisfy your perception of who Jesus
    was, is? Discuss each of the three positions stated above.

6. How would you describe Jesus? What elements of His being
    are most important to you? Why?

Resurrection

How exciting it was to be at the Naval Academy Chapel again.
This was the third time in five years that we were having a
wedding ceremony there for a family member. Five years
earlier, Michael and Cheryl married there just two weeks following Michael's graduation from the Academy. The year before
our niece married there. And now it was our daughter,
Stephanie, marrying a graduating ensign.

It was such a happy time. We traveled to Annapolis to spend the
week-end at the Maryland House, a restored eighteenth century
inn, just off Church Circle in the heart of town. The festivities
around the wedding captured the attention of everyone in town.
Yvonne had put together quite an affair. No one could have ever
believed that an all-white wedding could be so stunning.
Through Yvonne's effort and planning, everything went off like
clockwork. It was surely a wonderful start for a young, happy
couple. Who could have known what was lurking only one
month away?

Stephanie's husband, Glen, had accepted an education billet for
three months in Mexico. Yvonne expressed her concern about
going there. She almost begged Stephanie not to go. But this
was to be a wonderful honeymoon for them, a great experience
of being in another country. Stephanie told us that this was a
chance to travel, to study a language in another country, to see
another culture firsthand, to experience another lifestyle. This
was the purpose. But something went wrong; dreadfully wrong.
We still do not know the full story. It took Stephanie seven years
to give us insight into some of the events that occurred on that
adventure. Let me share with you a letter she wrote recently:

> "Glen and I were supposedly off on the rare and exciting
> adventure of our lifetime. I was really thrilled — a little
> scared, but fearless just the same.

"As circumstance would have it, this adventure turned to disaster; tragedy on a weekend jaunt to Puerto Varta, Mexico. It was a time to celebrate our one month anniversary. It happened so quickly. I was abducted by two Mexican men. They grabbed me as I crossed the alleyway between two buildings. They bashed my head against the wall until I fell unconscious. I awoke on a very long, very deserted beach. Water was near; there were rocks all around, especially near my head. I was feeling fuzzy, constantly bordering on a loss of consciousness. My eyesight was blurred; my body hurt bad. I was unclear as to what they had exactly already done to me. I felt an emotion unsurpassed by any emotion I have ever experienced, ever!

"In the hours that passed, I was subject to the most brutal, degrading, most sickening acts. I was terrorized, violated, brutalized both sexually and mentally. There I was, thinking, praying, desperately trying to figure a way out. How could I get away? I was outnumbered, overpowered, incapacitated physically. Then, finally, I was able to hurt them a little. They decided I should die. I could hear them jabbering in the foreign tongue that I had been listening to for hours. But I knew! They dragged me down to the water. The tide was coming in. I pretended to be unconscious. They turned me face down into the water. I still pretended to be unconscious.

"The little waves were splashing on me. The water wasn't that deep yet. I blew tiny breaths to make a small pocket in the sand. As the water moved back, I could get a little breath of air. Oh how I needed the water to move back! I faked being dead. Seeing me lifeless like that must have scared my assailants. They were more scared than expected and ran off."

The letter from Stephanie was unfinished. It was all she could write. It was much more than she had been able to face over the past seven years. There is more to the story locked within the tormented memories of my daughter. I will not press her for the details.

I still remember the time that we found out about the attack. Yvonne and I sensed that something was wrong. We enlisted a neighbor's daughter-in-law that knew Spanish to help us track down Stephanie. I remember her first comments saying that she was attacked. I felt helpless and violated. Yet how much more so did Stephanie feel that pain. We insisted that they come home immediately and anxiously awaited the time just to see her and try to comfort her. We met her and Glen at the airport. She was different. We all were different. My heart cried out to her. My first instinctive response was to seek revenge, but then I realized how un-Christian that was. Yet the hate was there. My healing would come much quicker than Stephanie's.

In discussing this with Stephanie, I asked her what impact it had on her life. She told me the following:

"You need to know that evil and the devil exists to know that God exists. That awful experience told me of the evil in the world. You had so protected me from that in the past. But that set me to seek the good, and God. There is no doubt in my mind that God sent Jesus to balance out the evil and that Jesus was resurrected for my salvation."

Stephanie sees that event as being a turning point in her life. It was the beginning of a change that would bring her ever closer to her God. Before that, she could not know what evil meant. Before that, she could not know that God was active in her daily life. Before that, she was not willing to turn herself over to God.

The road to spirituality was a long road. She did not change that very day. It took time to consider the circumstances. It took time to consider the cause of the problem. It took time to consider the hurt and embarrassment. Stephanie is not over the incident. She has much to reconcile, much to face, much to

overcome. But for her, the incident at the beach was a really
new beginning. A true resurrection from a life of despair. A new
beginning from some wanderings in the search for independence.

The years following have not been kind. There were more trials
and tribulations for her. But, she found on that beach an ability
to rise from the ashes of despair. She found an inner strength
that she didn't know she possessed. She began a healing that
continues this day. Is Stephanie over the trauma? Certainly not.
Is she recovering? Most assuredly! The source of her recovery
is the new found faith in God and her desire to overcome all evil
that confronts her in her life.

This experience of Stephanie's was the closest thing to a resurrection that I have known. There was sorrow for what she had
been through, yet there is joy at where she is today. She was
always a fragile, china doll, yet she is now strong and independent. She was left for dead, but she is alive.

The single-most important event recorded in the Bible is the
resurrection of Jesus Christ. For me it speaks of God's love and
firmly establishes my hope. It is a demonstration of continuing
existence that gives meaning to my life.

The resurrection of Jesus is well documented. He appeared to
individuals, to small groups and to a crowd of more than 500
followers. This was not a fantasy story contrived by a couple of
Jesus' followers. It was an actual event with many eye wit-
nesses. There are indeed many doubting Thomas' in this world.
I do not need to see the risen Lord. The evidence is convincing
to me. Following are the Biblical references of Jesus' appearances after the crucifixion.

POST-RESURRECTION
APPEARANCES OF JESUS

"who through the Spirit of holiness was declared with power to be the Son of God by his resurrection from the dead: Jesus Christ our Lord." (Ro. 1:4)

Scene	Reference
To Mary Magdalene at the sepulcher	John 20:11-18 Mark 16:9
To certain women as they return from the sepulcher after the angel told them He has risen	Matthew 28:9
To Peter before the evening of the day of the resurrection	Luke 24:34 1 Corinthians 15:5
To two disciples (Cleopas and another) on the way to Emmaus on the afternoon of the resurrection	Mark 16:14-16 Luke 24:15-31
To ten apostles (possibly with others) assembled for the evening meal on the day of the resurrection	Mark 16:14-18 Luke 24:36-40 John 20:19-24
To the eleven apostles one week after the resurrection probably at the same place as the previous appearance	John 20:26-28
To seven disciples while they were fishing at the Sea of Galilee	John 21:1-14
To the eleven apostles on a mountain in Galilee	Matthew 28:16-17
To more than 500 hundred followers at the same time	1 Corinthians 15:6
To James	1 Corinthians 15:7
To the apostles at Jerusalem immediately before the ascension from the Mount of Olives, forty days after the resurrection	Mark 16:19 Luke 24:50-52 Acts 1:2-9
To Saul (Paul) on the road to Damascus, several years after the resurrection	Acts 9:1-6 1 Corinthians 15:8

Milestone #12

Experience the living presence of a resurrected Jesus.

1. Books on near-death experiences have been very poplar recently. Have you known anyone that claimed such an experience? Discuss the significant sights, sounds, feelings that are part of these experiences from what you have read, heard, or understood?

2. There is scientific evidence that people have been declared clinically dead on an operating table yet have come back to life. What explanation do you have for such possibilities? Do you believe that God had a role in those cases? If so, what role and how was it enacted?

3. Is the resurrection of Jesus important to your faith? Why?

4. Read John 20:24-29. Discuss the attitude of Thomas before the appearance of Jesus. How does this compare with his attitude after he has seen Jesus? What message do you get from Jesus' comments to Thomas?

5. Jesus was crucified as a sacrifice for my sins. Jesus rose from the dead to demonstrate the hope of eternal life to the children of God. Are these statements true? Would you change them in any way? How and why? Is one statement more important to you than the other? Why?

6. Has Jesus demonstrated His living presence to you in any way? If so, describe how and discuss the impact on your life.

Eternally Existing

In 1973, Yvonne and I made our first trip to Europe. It was a trip to Rome, the Eternal City. That trip has become one of our finest memories. It was a glorious eight days. We were so much in awe of Rome that we didn't take the time for any excursions to other localities, such as Venice and Florence. One thought kept recurring in my mind: Here is history of more than two thousand years woven into the present day.

Here is the Rome of triumph with its emperors and princes, the Rome of Christianity with its martyrs and popes, the Rome of Renaissance with its patrons and artists. It is an ever-present city with unending rebirth. The ruins of all the previous Romes are intermingled with the present, what the Romans call "Terza Rome", the third Rome.

One can sense the mythical beginnings of Rome as a she-wolf rescues Remus and Romulus from the Tiber River and raises them to become the founders of the first Rome. One can see remains of the wall of Servius Tullis that surrounded the fabled seven hills of Rome. This wall was completed in the sixth century B.C. and has a backdrop of twentieth century architecture. It is not difficult to imagine the strength of the fortified Rome of almost three thousand years ago.

The aqueducts, public baths and roadways speak of the creative ingenuity of Imperial Rome. The Pantheon, Colosseum, Marcellus Theater, Circus Maximus, Forum Romanum all give a feeling of grandeur of the time of the emperors. Imposing monuments and statues give life to the Caesars, Trajan, Hadrian and Marcus Arelius.

The most well known and probably the most popular of the ancient ruins is the Colosseum. As we stood within the walls, I could almost hear the ancient crowds shouting their cheers and jeers at the combatant gladiators. Then I realized why this place was so popular. This place has become the very symbol of the transformation of the Roman Empire from paganism to Christianity. The cries of those early Christian martyrs rise to the heavens and overcome the shouts of the spectators.

When we visited the Forum Romanum, I just wandered among the ruins and imagined the hustle and bustle of the ancient Romans in the marketplace, at the steps of the assembly hall, and along the paved streets. It was as if I were mingling among the ancient crowds, philosophizing about the meaning of life, listening to the oracles of learned men, participating in small groups theorizing about political issues, jumping from the path of horse-drawn chariots. There at the end of the forum I saw the Arch of Titus. Beyond the Arch lies one of the seven hills, mount Palatine. This monument was in excellent condition. It was built to commemorate the capture of Jerusalem in 70 A.D. My thoughts raced to the prophecy of Jesus on the fall of Jerusalem and the destruction of the Temple.

Later we found ourselves on the Via Appia, the Appian Way. Now I could see the legions of Roman soldiers marching out to the Orient under the command of Constantine. Passing the catacombs, one must contemplate the two centuries of use by the early Christians as they dug these tunnels and caves to conceal their meeting places, burial grounds and hideaways. But Constantine presses on to establish Christianity as the world's religion. His dedication to demonstrate this change in the Empire led to the capital being moved from Rome to Constantinople.

Then in a time-warp leap of more than a millennium, one admires the accomplishments of the great artists of the Renaissance. Every few steps brings wonder as you stop to take in the beauty, the strength, of these works of art that abound on, in and around the important buildings of this ageless city. The Spanish Steps leading from the Piazza di Spagna to the baroque church, Trinità dei Monti, are a favorite meeting place for the artists of

today, as they have been for centuries. Fountains by Bernini
appear in many of the piazzas. At the church, San Peitro, in
Vincoli is an impressive marble statute of Moses by
Michelangelo. One cannot pass by this statue without stopping
to gaze upon it, study it, contemplate it and recall Michelangelo
saying that the image is already within the marble just waiting to
be released by him.

The culmination of the Renaissance is made visible at St. Peter's
Basilica and Square in the Vatican. Words cannot express the
magnificence of these edifices of man being raised to God.
Michaelangelo's strong Moses would fit in with the large, almost
overbearing artwork and architecture at St. Peter's. This now is all
in contrast to the gentle, compassionate figures in the Pietà by
Michelangelo. Like everyone else, I was spell bound with the
frescoes of the Sistine Chapel. The museums of the Vatican contain
all types of art work of known and unknown artists from all over the
world; an accumulation across the history of Christianity. The
symbols and representations of the Christian faith can be found
there for anyone to enjoy and to contemplate. Those expressions in
paint, marble, tapestry, writings, architecture brought new awareness to me of the basic concepts in my faith.

Now we move into the twentieth century. We walked from our
hotel along the Via Veneto to do some casual shopping. In
talking to shopkeepers, we were directed to shopping areas off
the tourists route and some eating places that were favorites for
the locals, having already eaten at Alfredo's and other popular
eateries. On one of those jaunts, we found ourselves at the
Ristorante Tavernelle, a small restaurant on Via Panisperna. The
owner was our waiter. As we struggled with our communication,
we finally gave in to the owner serving us what he thought we
would like. It turned out to be multiple courses and covered
everything imaginable. We were truly filled to the brim when
the chef came out to inquire about our satisfaction with the meal.
Somehow, our gestures got the message across that we were very
pleased. The owner, chef and other restaurant employees

gathered around us and sang to us in Italian. We joined in with the few words we could say. Our meal experience went on for about three hours. It was a wonderfully fun experience and became a lasting memory of the kindness and hospitality of the Romans.

It was apparent to me that the secret of Rome was its ability to absorb from other cultures and continually modify their own culture. To me, Rome has always been there; at least the spirit of Rome has. The absorbsion of early Estrucan culture, the modification of Greek mythology, the expansion of the Oriental trading practices, the transition to a mid-Eastern religion all reflect the flexibility that enabled continuing survival. But more importantly Rome gave back to the world. Its expansionist thrust shared all that it was with the rest of the then-known world. Even more, though, Rome added to what it had absorbed its own qualities of logic, organization and massive construction. Rome did not take; it absorbed. Rome did not destroy, it shared and built. The rebuilding of ruins — stone upon stone, culture upon culture — demonstrares this within its own walls. Rome, the spirit of Rome, will always be there.

This doesn't nearly capture all that there is to say concerning our trip to Rome. Our understanding can only be a small immeasurable view of that Eternal City. The time came for us to say, "Arriverderci Roma", and as most tourist, we tossed our coin over our shoulder into the Fontana di Trevi to ensure that we would see Rome again someday.

Certainly, empires had existed long before the Roman Empire. The Egyptian and Assyrian empires, as well as the Oriental Dynasties, can trace their histories to two thousand years before Rome. Possibly it is because I have been to Rome and seen and touched the artifacts that it holds the impression of being eternal. But I think that it is more. The Roman Empire brought together the East and the West. It absorbed much from the Eastern cultures and gave to them much in return. Roman presence could be seen around all of the then known world. Rome grew from the passive contributor to the death of Christ, to the aggressive suppresser of the Christian movement, to the champion of the Christian faith. So to me, Rome is the "Eternal City". It has, for me, always existed, and will continue to exist.

God has always existed. He goes beyond space, time and matter. These are all subject to His creativity. So too, Jesus has always existed, and He is eternally the same. As the second person in the Trinity, Jesus is God. He has always been there. For a brief period of time he was on earth in the manifestation of the man Jesus, but as the Christ deity, He has always been at the right hand of the Father. The prophets of old knew that Jesus was there at the beginning. The apostles wrote of Jesus being before and after His earthly existence. Jesus tells us that He was there before Abraham and will await us in the heavenly kingdom; His healing presence is obvious in my life and is known by my heart.

The following table reflects some of the Biblical evidence to support this:

The Ever-Present Jesus

"Jesus Christ is the same yesterday and today and forever." (Hebrews 13:8)

Evidence	Reference	Text
Jesus fulfills the prophets	Micah 5:2	But you, Bethlehem Ephrathah, though you are small among the clans of Judah, out of you will come for me one who will be ruler over all Israel, whose origins are from of old, from ancient times.
	John 8:58	"I tell you the truth," Jesus answered, "before Abraham was born, I am!"
Jesus is the Word	John 1:1-2	In the beginning was the Word, and the Word was with God, and the Word was God. He was with God in the beginning.
Jesus the binding force	Colossians 1:17	He is before all things, and in him all things hold together.
Jesus is glorified	John 17:24	"Father, I want those you have given me to be with me where I am, and to see my glory, the glory you have given me because you loved me before the creation of the world."
Jesus is the eternal priest	Hebrews 7:3	Without father or mother, without genealogy, without beginning of days or end of life, like the Son of Man he remains a priest forever.
Jesus is our salvation	2Timothy 1:9	who has saved us and called us to a holy life---not because of anything we have done but because of his own purpose and grace. This grace was given to us in Christ Jesus before the beginning of time.

Milestone #13

Know that Jesus is here today, has always been here, and always will be.

1. Have you ever said of anyone that they have always been there for you? Who was that individual? What made you feel that they were always there?

2. What would be the impact on your life if that person wasn't there for you tomorrow?

3. Has anyone ever said to you that you have always been there for them? If so, what did that mean to you? How did you feel about that? Did you consider it an imposed responsibility? Once that is said to you, do you feel there is, or would be, a change in relationship to that person? Explain.

4. Read John 17:5. What does this verse mean to you?

5. Read Psalm 102:24-27. How does this compare to Hebrews 13:8?

6. How important is it to you to believe that Jesus has always been and will always be? How does this impact on what you do today?

Purpose

Man's Purpose

There are a group of books in the Bible called the Wisdom Books. These include Job, Proverbs and Ecclesiastes. In looking through these books one can find a searching for meaning and the very purpose of life.

"Utterly meaningless! Everything is meaningless. What does man gain from all his labor at which he toils under the sun?" (Ecclesiastes 1:2-3). Most everyone is familiar with the phrase from this book, "chasing after the wind". The writer states all of the pursuits in life and after each comments that they are meaningless, like chasing after the wind. Can it be that all we do has no meaning? Can it be that there is no purpose in this life?

"A man can do nothing better than to eat and drink and find satisfaction in his work. This too, I see, is from the hand of God, for without him, who can eat and find enjoyment?" (Ecclesiastes 2:24-25). The writer found it necessary to repeat this thought several times throughout the book. This sounds much like the modern cliché, "Eat, drink and be merry for tomorrow you may die!" Can it be that the writer only saw the purpose of our creation was to enjoy ourselves? I believe that God wants us to be happy and find enjoyment, but our circumstances and our choices in life are barriers to fulfilling that plan.

I recall that, as a young man, I had dreams of doing something significant, something that meant something. There wasn't anything specific in mind, just a desire to make things better. In reflection, I see that what I really meant by making things better was to make them better for me. I moved through young adulthood knowing that tomorrow would, in fact, be better: a better education, a better job, a better home, a better car, and so on.

As I grew into the roles of husband and father, there was a transference from better for me to better for my family. Since I was part of "my family", I hadn't lost all sense of selfishness. Being involved in the activities of my children focused my attention on making their quality of life as good as I possibly could. That involvement directed me to attempt to change the circumstances of life to make them as favorable as possible for my children. Yvonne and I worked together on many of these efforts. This included changing the process for appointing members to the local Board of Education, changing policies for selecting books for the local libraries, reassigning teachers, changing practices in the schools and community sports organizations, providing input to local politics and challenging local legislation. It seemed that everything I got involved with resulted in some crusade to make a change, and this carried over into the church and work environments.

Much of the change that came about as a result of my efforts, and those of my wife, did not benefit our children though. It takes time for change to happen. We had to be content with the knowledge that others would benefit from the action and not be subject to the unfair condition that we saw. It is as if we had become "change agents". As soon as we got deeply involved in something, we saw a need to make some sort of change and we set at the task of making that change possible. Our real purpose for the involvement in the first place was to enjoy the benefits of the association or activity. There was no conceived plan to get involved to make changes. Soon we found that many people were coming to us requesting that we get involved in some activity and make the changes they wanted. It seems that others viewed our purpose as one to make change.

Somewhere along the way, Yvonne and I both burned out. We began avoiding all involvement. By this time our children were pretty much grown and on their own. Now I was what the calendar calls a mature adult. I had come of age. It was then natural for me to reflect on all those activities, all that energy, and to ask myself, "What did it really accomplish?" It was a time to become philosophical about my life. As I withdrew from the involvement in all those activities, the meaning of my life seemed to be unclear. Like the writer of Ecclesiastes, I questioned what had really been accomplished and did it have any meaning. Was I just chasing after the wind? It was almost as though the very act of questioning of the meaning of life hid the meaning.

Today I look back and realize that all that involvement, all that activity, all that spent energy, all that turmoil created a very high level of happiness in my life. We could look for the psychological reasons, but it seems to me to be as simple as finding satisfaction in "all" that I was doing. Being involved with family and friends added to that satisfaction. Now as I reactivate my faith I am finding that same level of happiness.

"Now all has been heard; here is the conclusion of the matter; fear God and keep his commandments, for this is the whole duty of man, for God will bring every deed into judgment, including every hidden thing, whether it is good or bad." (Ecclesiastes 12:13-14). God indeed meant us to be happy. He provides opportunity in every one of life's situations to find that satisfaction and happiness. It is our attitude to those situations, the choices we make in those situations, the effort we put into those situations that determines the level of our happiness.

In the story of creation, we read that God's good earth was relinquished to man as a gift. God's first words to man were, "I give you....." (Genesis 1:29-30, 2:9,18). Scripture declares that the Heavenly Father fashioned His world in terms of His children's needs, and when all was ready man inherited the earth. This gift, however, came with responsibility, or purpose.

Man's Responsibility

Purpose	Reference	Responsibility
Replenish the earth	Genesis 1:28	God is seeking to share his creative capacities. We are called to participate in an ongoing creative venture. Life must bring forth life.
Subdue the earth	Genesis 1:28	This rich world offers the full measure of its blessings and benefits, only insofar as we use all our powers to develop and appropriate what is here. We are to probe, search, discover and utilize all the earth's rich fruits. The domain on which we live waits to be mastered.
Dress, till and keep the earth	Genesis 2:15	We must have deep concern as to how we use the earth. We must seek to protect and preserve that which is precious so all generations of God's children will enjoy the good bounties of the land.
Have dominion over the earth	Genesis 1:28	All things of the earth are put under man's feet. The lower forms of life are subject to man.

When God next speaks to man, He limits man's freedom, "...but you must not eat from the tree of the knowledge of good and evil..." (Genesis 2:16-17). Even in this wonderful society in the United States, our liberty brings with it certain responsibilities and limitations in freedom. Thankfully, we are in a country that provides the amount of freedom that we do have.

The third time God speaks to man, it reflects man's separation from God. "But the Lord called to the man, 'Where are you?'" (Genesis 3:9). By not living up to our responsibilities, and accepting our limitations, we are separated from God. The scriptures reveal how swift that separation can occur. When separated from God, we are separated in fellowship, not relationship. We are still God's children.

Milestone #14

Take on your responsibility to be a child of God.

1. Identify the activities you are involved in within the community and church. How did you become involved in each? Why are you, or were you, involved?

2. What were the most significant accomplishments that you are proud of from your community and church involvement? What impact did these accomplishments have on others? Why are you so proud of them?

3. Have you ever wondered about your purpose in life? Define what you believe that purpose to be? Are you doing what you believe you should be doing? Why, or why not?

4. Have you set goals for achieving your purpose in life? If so, what are those goals? What are the barriers to achieving those goals? What are the enablers?

5. Do you believe your goals are in harmony with God's will? Describe your belief and feelings on this.

6. What do you consider to be your most significant talent(s)? Define stewardship. Do you consider yourself a good steward of your time, talents and resources? Are you making the best use of the blessings Gad has granted you? If so, how? If not, why not?

Jesus' Mission

Our daughter, Stephanie, has worked in many different environments and held a variety of positions: including general office, public relations and sales. But the activities she most enjoys are those that have one-on-one relationships. She has worked in nursing homes and perfomed home care for an autistic, handicapped young man. Presently she works in a private care center for the mentally and physically handicapped.

At those times in her life when she has worked with the aged or handicapped, she has seemed to be at her happiest. There is an enthusiasm in all she does, even though the work is most demanding. I look back on her life and recall how she was always bringing home a stray animal, or showing special friendship to someone that had no other friends. She was particularly helpful and charming with older people and bonded closely with her grandparents.

Time and again, I would have talks with her about the friends she chose. Generally her response to me was, "But Pop, they don't have anyone else; they need me!" I would make some shallow comment in return, like, "You can't take on all the problems of the world." In any event, I never really had much influence on her selection of friends.

She is always reaching out to help someone, or some cause. At times she would barely have enough money to buy food, yet she was supporting some child in a far away country or contributing to some animal protection society. Without question, she is a very caring person and always anxious to help.

Each day she cheerfully goes to work with an attitude of making a difference. She sees pain and suffering and tragedy each day, yet she continues to reflect joy to all those she is helping. I can say with conviction that the handicapped individuals she attends to sense the honest love and concern she has for them. They are continually calling out for her.

Stephanie is always on the alert for something that may interest her residents at the care center. At Christmas time she took two van-loads of residents to a local Christmas shop to see the displays and bright lights. That was followed by a stop at a restaurant. She plans trips for them to the park, or the museum, or some local point of interest. For some, it would be too much trouble to deal with the wheelchairs, the child-like questions and actions, the unexpected reaction to the unknown. But for Stephanie, she sees the potential joy her residents would get from the experience so the effort is worth it.

Each day Stephanie comes home from work anxious to talk about the fun things that she did with the residents. She is radiant, enthusiastic, and happy. This is more then her chosen work; this work has chosen her and given her purpose.

The Reason for Jesus

"For God did not send his Son into the world to condemn the world, but to save the world through him." (John 3:17)

Reason	Reference	Text
Sinfulness of mankind	Ro. 3:23	"for all have sinned and fall short of the glory of God."
Sin results in death	Ro. 6:23	"For the wages of sin is death, but the gift of God is eternal life in Christ Jesus our Lord."
Demonstration of God's love	Ro. 5:8	"But God demonstrates his own love for us in this: While we were still sinners, Christ died for us."
Fulfill the law and prophecies	Mt. 5:17	"Do you think I have come to abolish the Law or the Prophets; I have not come to abolish them but to fulfill them."
Provides a way to God	Jn. 14:6	"I am the way and the truth and the life. No one comes to the Father except through me."
Be the mediator	1 Ti. 2:25	"For there is one God and one mediator between God and men, the man Christ Jesus."

God looked down on the state of mankind and had compassion.
He knew that we could not, by our own effort, ever achieve
fellowship with Him. A great chasm had been created by
mankind's sinfulness. Throughout ancient history, God had
attempted to guide mankind to live in perfect harmony with Him.
Adam and Eve started a trend that was spiralling toward eternal
damnation. The great flood only slowed the coming doom. The
direct issuance of laws, such as The Ten Commandments, had
only a temporary effect. The empowered judges, time and again,
rescued a defeated people. The enlightened prophets warned of
penalties brought by evil ways. The anointed kings were seldom
pure enough to lead the people.

God needed to take the next major step in the redemptive plan.
He had to give His people a way to have communion with Him;
a way to join Him in eternal peace. The great task required a
great judge, prophet, king and teacher. His gift would become a
sacrifice. A sacrifice that Abraham did not have to make, but
one that He knew must be made: His Son.

Milestone #15

Understand that Jesus came to save the world from sin.

1. Describe the most memorable sacrifice you have had to make for someone else, whether spouse, child, parent, friend, neighbor, co-worker, or stranger. What need were you attempting to satisfy? Why did you make the sacrifice? Did the sacrifice accomplish what you intended? If not, why not?

2. What inconvenience, or price, did this sacrifice cost you? How did you feel about the cost to you of that sacrifice? Would you be willing to do this again? Why, or why not? What, if anything, would you have done differently?

3. How appreciative was the individual(s) that received benefit from your sacrifice? How did they demonstrate that appreciation?

4. Did your sacrifice have a temporary or permanent impact on individuals, family, or community? Explain.

5. What was Jesus' purpose in coming into this world? Did He achieve that purpose? How? Was the impact temporary or long-lasting? Why?

6. What benefit have you received from Jesus' sacrifice? Why is that important to you? How do you show your appreciation?

Man's Commission

As a family we were blessed with the ownership of a condominium on the Atlantic Ocean in Maryland. Through the years we had many happy moments there. Those were happy times for each of us, for all of us. It was a special time of sharing. I previously discussed the impact of just going to the ocean had on me.

That ocean was like a tranquilizer for me from the fast-paced, super-active life style of an involved family. Whenever we got within a few miles of the ocean, there was a sudden transformation in me. The tasks to be done at work fell away. The struggle to be competitive was no longer important. The pressures of assumed and imposed responsibilities were lifted. My attitude was lively and care-free. Most of the family used their time at the ocean for relaxation, playing in the surf and sand and socializing with friends. But Michael got involved with the activities of the sea. He went fishing and boating. He also worked with commercial fishermen and spent time with the local leisure fishermen. He kept us in a steady supply of fish for our meals. Michael's love for the sea grew stronger with each trip. He loved and enjoyed the ocean more than his brother or sister.

By comparison, I loved the ocean for the comfort it brought me; for the opportunity to contemplate the ever changing surface; for the joy of bringing the family together. My love of the ocean was a passive love compared to Michael's. He loved being in union with the ocean; being involved; giving to and taking from the ocean. His was an active love. It was that active love that reinforced his desire to work on the sea and to go to the Naval Academy.

It was a happy day when Michael went to the Academy, but even a happier day when he graduated. But it was a day that started with great anxiety. Michael had a hunting accident in his last year at the Academy. He fell out of a tree stand from about 30 feet and injured his back. Two vertebrae were crushed. Because of this, Michael could not perform certain physical tests required to be commissioned into the Navy. Time was drawing near to graduation and Michael was advised that he would not be approved for jet pilot training because of the back injury. It was a certainty that he would graduate, but a commission as an officer in the Navy was in jeopardy. He was interviewed for the nuclear submarine program, but he had not heard if he would be accepted or even if he would receive a commission. The last physical test was successfully completed by him just days before graduation.

From the stands, we anxiously awaited for the graduating class to march on. Finally, we caught sight of Michael and he gave us the high-sign that he was being commissioned. What a relief! And so, he did receive his commission.

"I, Michael Johnson, having been appointed an ensign in the United States Navy, do solemnly affirm that I will support and defend the Constitution of the United States against all enemies, foreign and domestic; that I will bear true faith and allegiance to the same; that I take this obligation freely, without any mental reservation or purpose of evasion; and that I will well and faithfully discharge the duties of the office of which I am about to enter: So help me God."

 Michael was selected to be a member of an elite group. He was trained to perform the duties of the office. He didn't know where or how he would serve until he was actually given the commission. After a dozen years, he still serves his country proudly, willingly, and faithfully.

Now let us look at another graduating class. This class enthusiastically waited for the ceremony to begin. They looked forward to the keynote speaker's address. And they were filled with anxiety for the unknown that lay before them. Where would their new vocation take them? What position of authority, or rank, would they hold? How were they to perform their assigned duties?

It was a small group, only eleven men made it to the commissioning ceremony. Thousands had wanted to be part of this elite group. Only twelve were selected for the three-year training course. One of those did not qualify for graduation. As Michael had received his command to go and serve his country, so this small group was about to receive their "Go Command". It is known as The Great Commission, and it resulted in a tradition of service that has continued for nearly two thousand years.

The Great Commission
Matthew 28:16-20

Text	Condition
Then the eleven disciples went to Galilee, to the mountain where Jesus told them to go.	Obedience to Christ
When they saw him, they worshipped him,	Christ is worshipped
but some doubted.	Had doubts
Then Jesus came to them, and said,	The Commander comes
"All authority in heaven and earth has been given to me.	Evidence of authority, power
Therefore go and make disciples of all nations,	The go command
baptizing them in the name of the Father and of the Son and of the Holy Spirit,	Instruction to baptize
and teaching them to obey everything I have commanded you.	Instruction to teach
And surely I will be with you always, to the very end of the age."	Divine presence, inseparable

This commission has been passed down through the ages to each of us. It is the maturing of the commands to "love your neighbor" and to "serve others". When we are obedient to Christ, our doubts and questions are overcome. We are given the authority and direction for our commission. And this all is with the assurance of His everliving presence amongst us.

Milestone #16

Share what you have been taught with others.

1. What person stands out in your memory as your most important mentor or teacher? Why? What impact has that had on your life?

2. How did that person go about mentoring, or teaching, you? Do you feel you received special attention? Why?

3. Describe a situation where you feel you have been in the role of a mentor or teacher. How did you feel about performing that role? Has anyone recognized you as their special mentor or teacher (this could include a younger sibling or your own child)?

4. What do you feel is the motivation for mentoring or teaching others?

5. Have you had special training for certain specific skills? Identify those skills and the training received. Was that training required by your employer, your own desire, other influences? Why was it required? Once the skill was learned did you want to keep it to yourself or share it with others to help them? Explain.

6. Is it possible for a Christian to live, by choice, as a hermit? Are there circumstances that you feel it is necessary for a Christian to live as a hermit? Discuss.

Promise

The Old Covenant

I grew up with the sense that education was very important. My Father completed 3½ years of college. He never went back to get a degree and he never pursued his desire to be a history teacher. My Mother never graduated from high school. Yet both of them instilled in me the desire for an advanced, formal education.

My maternal grandparents had a prized possession. It was a set of "Collier's National Encyclopedia and Harvard Classics." These books were kept in a glass-doored curio cabinet and prominently displayed in their sitting room. I do not ever recall seeing them reading from these books, but I certainly had the impression that they were very important to them. Generally, on my visits to their home I would occupy myself by reading from these books. It was certainly unusual, within our circle of acquaintances, for a ten-year old to be reading from the Harvard Classics. At that early age, I did not have a full understanding of what I was reading, but I know that I was enjoying the reading. My imagination would soar as my thoughts adapted, modified and enhanced the words before me. When my grandparents passed away, I was given the books. Over the years, I have gone to those books often to re-read the classics. Perhaps my imagination is less active now, but the same feeling of awe comes upon me as I read from one of the great writers of the past. These books are still a proud possession. They have a predominate place on my bookshelves.

When I graduated from high school, I had several scholastic and athletic scholarships offered to me. I was living with my parents, but I had been basically self-supporting during those high school years. There wasn't room and board to pay, but everything else was covered by the various jobs I had that fit in with my school and sports schedule. My parents were doing little more than making ends meet. It seemed unfair to have them support me through college. I chose to begin my career by going to work full time and attending night school for my education. I was able to convert one of my scholastic scholarships to a night school program. It was a long and arduous effort to pursue my undergraduate and graduate studies in this manner. I did not want my children to have to do likewise.

From very early in our marriage, Yvonne and I both felt that the only real legacy we could pass on to our children was the best possible education that we could provide for them. This was the motivation behind our involvement in their school activities. In each and every school that our children attended, teachers, counselors and administrators knew we were ready to be involved for the benefit of our child. Few understood the tenacity of our involvement. They did not realize that Yvonne and I had made a silent covenant to our children to educate them in the best possible way.

Our involvement continued when they went on to college. Keeping that promise for a good education was sometimes difficult. I remember the great joy we had when Bruce was accepted to attend Johns Hopkins. The difficulty was that tuition and boarding costs amounted to approximately one-third of my annual gross income at the time. Somehow, we managed to bear that financial burden for the four years of the undergraduate program. We never looked at that as a burden, and we certainly never lacked for any of the perceived necessities of a comfortable life. In fact, on reflection, it seems we had more money when we didn't have any money.

With the promise to our children for a good education, there was an obligation attached. They were to do the best they could do. This was not to be measured in their placement in the graduating class or the grades they got in each course. It was measured in their desire and effort. Subjective as these measurements were, as parents, we were able to effectively measure this in our children.

Bruce did his best, but we disagreed with his priorities. As a freshman, he made the varsity baseball and soccer teams and participated in numerous intramural sports. Bruce's dream was to be a major league pitcher, and he worked hard towards that goal. He was chosen the outstanding pitcher on Johns Hopkins team in his freshman and sophomore years, and was on a pace to set school records in wins, strikeouts and complete games. I attended the games that I could, and became increasingly concerned about the ability of the coach. His warm-ups were not proper for a pitcher, there was not adequate rest between games, and he was required to throw many curve balls with a young arm. Bruce began experiencing frequent back and arm pain and it got worse with each year. The dream of his youth was beginning to fade.

While all this was going on, Bruce was interested in the newly discovered social activities. It was just one week after Bruce's seventeenth birthday that we took him to his dormitory room to begin his advanced education. The literature left on his desk for him to read brought an unexpected awareness to us. The warnings concerning social diseases and pregnancy out of wedlock fell on Yvonne and me like a brick. Our son was a young man about to be exposed to those things that we suddenly felt we had not prepared him for properly. The next couple of years, Bruce demonstrated that he was not quite ready for the changes that were about to occur. He always resisted regimentation and discipline, but the advanced college courses selected required these attitudes to be self-imposed and self-enforced to maintain the necessary focus. And now he had the opportunity to participate in any and all sports, whether on varsity, intramural, or make-up teams. Bruce spent more time in the gym than he did in the classroom.

All of this diverted his attention and his grades began to show it. In keeping with our pattern of involvement, we met with the coaches, counselors, professors and administrators. The result was that we insisted that Bruce not participate in varsity baseball, his curriculum was changed, and he came home more frequently on weekends in his last two years. Bruce's willingness to readjust his priorities allowed him to graduate from Johns Hopkins. He then fulfilled his obligation.

We knew that if our children completed their education at the right institution they would be successful in their careers, and more importantly, in their life in general. It was an easy prophecy to make.

There is a covenant in the Old Testament. It is a covenant from God to an individual. It speaks to all the children that are to come and to each individual uniquely. I refer to it as "The Promise", for it is a promise from God. The promise of salvation. This is a legacy that God passes on to us. With the promise comes an obligation. It is an obligation that each of us can choose to take on through a willingness to be considered one of God's children. The following table reflects the elements of that covenant:

THE PROMISE
God's Covenant with Abraham

"I will make you into a great nation and I will bless you, I will make your name great, and you will be a blessing. I will bless those who bless you, and whoever curses you I will curse; and all peoples on earth will be blessed through you." (Genesis 12:1-3)

Old Testament Covenant		
Element	**Text**	**Meaning**
Promise	"I will bless you"	God's promises are the foundation blocks on which we can build our hopes. We have the right to dream big dreams.
Obligation	"So that you will be a blessing"	All good things received from God's hand must be turned into blessings for others. That which God invests in us is expected to be invested in others. No gift is to be hoarded.
Prophecy	"And all peoples on earth will be blessed by you"	Plans fashioned in God's mind will be fulfilled for His people.

The Old Testament covenant is directed to each of us. "The promise comes by faith, so that it may be by grace and may be guaranteed to all Abraham's offspring—not only to those who are of the law but also to those who are of the faith of Abraham. He is the father of us all." (Romans 4:16)

Milestone #17

Have faith in the promise that you will be blessed.

1. What does it mean to you to make a promise to someone? Do you believe you keep all promises you make? Why, or why not?

2. Do you know of anyone who makes you a promise and does not keep it? How does that impact you? What do you think of that person?

3. What does it mean to you to be blessed? Share with your group three blessings you have received.

4. Have you shared any of these blessings with others? If so, how and was it a voluntary sharing? If not, could you have shared them, and how would you have done so?

5. How would you compare your quality of life with your perception of the average American? With the average citizen of another Western civilization? With the average citizen of a Third World country?

6. Do you believe that God has blessed you? Explain. Does God bless everyone? What exceptions, if any, are there? Does God bless us equally? Explain your answer.

Other Old Testament Promises

The promise to give our children the best education possible was certainly a compelling one. It was not the only promise that I made to them. There were promises to love them forever, care for them always and protect them from all adversity. These promises are easily spoken or implied. As babies and small children, it was easy to fulfill those promises to them. Then, one day, they were all grown; they were making their own choices; they were no longer dependent on us for everything.

I have looked back and seen the times when I didn't provide for them in the manner I could have or protected them the way I thought I should have. However, I have never doubted the love that I have had for each of them. Perhaps the unfilled promises were from choices they made; perhaps from lack of persuasion from me; perhaps from choices I should have made. But those opportunities are past; they cannot be changed.

Wait! Those promises are not unfilled, they are yet to be filled. All the opportunities before me will allow me to fulfill what I have promised. There is no need to rethink what has been and what could have been done. It is time to prepare for tomorrow so that I can do all I promised, within my capabilities. It is time to build on those positive things that were done in the past.

There is a specific promise I recall making to each of our children. I told them that I would provide them with a car when they graduated from college. The promise wasn't for a new, top-of-the-line, fully equipped automobile, but rather a nice, clean means of transportation. In Bruce's case, we knew he wanted a new sports car, fully equipped. This was beyond our financial means at the time. Our compromise position was to put a substantial down payment on a new car and let Bruce assume the monthly payments since he had secured a very good job and was to begin work within a couple of weeks following graduation.

The excitement of graduation day was building within us. Yvonne and I looked forward to attending the ceremonies and seeing our first child receive his degree from a prestigious university. It was a sunny, warm, June day on the campus of Johns Hopkins. We were seated on metal folding chairs in the shade of a large canopy. It didn't matter that we were so far away from Bruce. We knew when he was on stage to receive his diploma. It didn't matter that perspiration was beaded on our foreheads. The excitement overcame our discomfort. It didn't matter that it was a struggle to keep him in this college. Our pride in Bruce lifted the sense of burden.

Following the ceremony, we searched the campus grounds until we found Bruce. After the hugs and kisses and tears and gleeful shouts, we gave Bruce his graduation present. We had put together an album that reflected all the activities of his last four years. It contained tuition invoices marked "Paid", grade average statements, pictures of the campus, family photographs, and much more. We made Bruce go through each page standing there on campus. He even had to read, out loud, the notes we wrote to him. The last page of the album had a picture of a new Ford Mustang with a set of keys. Early that morning I had driven to the campus and parked the car. Bruce had to walk around campus until he found a car that looked like the picture and a license that matched the tag on the keys. A half-hour later Bruce drove up with his new car. Now he was as happy as we were. Another small promise had been fulfilled.

In the previous chapter I briefly discussed the Old Covenant. The Old Testament contained many promises to the chosen people. The theme of the promises was really a further definition of the over riding promise of God to His people. These promises were made to a nation, to encourage and support that nation.

The following table is a selection of those promises that reflects a transition from being called as the chosen people to receiving the richness of God's unending mercy:

Promises to a Nation

Promise	Reference	Text
Chosen People	Exodus 6:7	"I will take you as my own people, and I will be your God. Then you will know that I an the Lord your God, who brought you out from under the yoke of the Egyptians."
Promised Land	Exodus 6:8	"And I will bring you to the land I swore with uplifted hand to give to Abraham, to Isaac and to Jacob. I will give it to you as a possession. I am the Lord."
Sins Forgiven	2 Chronicles 7:14	"If my people, who are called by my name, will humble themselves and pray and seek my face and turn from their wicked ways, then will I hear from heaven and will forgive their sin and will heal their land."
Protection	Psalm 138:7	"Though I walk in the midst of trouble, you preserve my life; you stretch out your hand against the anger of my foes, with your right hand you save me."
Not Hidden	Proverbs 8:17	"I love those who love me, and those who seek me find me."
Love	Joel 2:13	"Rend your heart and not your garments. Return to the Lord your God, for he is gracious and compassionate, slow to anger and abounding in love...."
Mercy	Micah 7:18	"Who is a God like you, who pardons sin and forgives the transgression of the remnant of his inheritance? You do not stay angry forever but delights to show mercy."

In these promises, I see a progression. It is the action of a caring God that is ever encouraging and supporting His people in steps they can understand. With each fall of the people, God lifts them up to even a higher level of the riches of His grace. All of these promises are but subsets of the original covenant God made with Abraham. And each of the promises leads to a new covenant.

Milestone #18

Obey God's commands and keep His covenant.

1. As God made promises to the Hebrew nation, did God attach conditions, or requirements, to the Hebrew people? If any, what were they? What is your interpretation of those conditions?

2. Read Exodus 19:5, Deuteronomy 4:40. What primary conditions are referred to in these verses? What does it mean to obey God? To keep God's commands?

3. Read Psalm 34:19. What does this verse mean to you? What promise does it contain? Is there a condition to this promise? Explain.

4. Read Proverbs 11:25. What does this verse mean to you? How does this compare with God's covenant to Abraham (Genesis 12:1-3)?

5. When you make a promise to someone else, is there an implied, or expressed, condition attached? Is there usually an obligation that is expected to be fulfilled? If someone makes a promise to you, do you feel you have an obligation to that person? Explain.

6. If you believe you are, or will be, blessed by God, what obligations do you feel you have, if any? Why? Are you fulfilling your obligations? If so, how? If not, why not?

The New Covenant

When I think of new promises, I think of the most important promise that I ever made. It is a promise that impacted my whole life. There are many important promises I have made over the years. The previous sections speaks of the promises to my children. There is also the promise I made to obey God's commandments, and the spoken and implied promises I have made to my employers. But the promise that I think of now is the promise I made to myself as a young teenager.

Every Friday night, the church had a social night for the teenagers. I usually attended, even though it often meant that I had to make arrangements to leave work early that one night of the week. This particular Friday night, I almost did not attend, but at the last moment my employer allowed me to leave early. The Friday night social was attended by all my friends, and new teenagers would often come. Some of them just came once and never returned. Others stayed on and often joined in other church activities. These Friday nights were filled with dancing to the latest tunes played on a 45 rpm record player. Also we played ping-pong and shuffle board. The church provided sodas and frequently someone would bring snacks. By today's standards this seems mild and boring, but all of my friends attended these Friday socials throughout their teenage years.

The night of my big promise started out as any other Friday social. I was busy participating in the games, talking over the events of the week and just having fun with my friends. Then, an acquaintance came in mid-way through the evening with a friend that was new to the group. Immediately this girl caught my fancy. I boldly asked her for a dance, and then another. After three or four dances, I had given this girl the complete history of my short life. While I don't recall what I said, I'm sure that I embellished my stories to impress this shy and beautiful young girl.

My cousin noticed her also and gave her some attention. I then
confided in my cousin the promise I had just moments ago made
to myself. "I am going to marry this girl." Obviously, this was
to let my cousin know that he better stay away from her. But it
was more. There was this overwhelming sense of having to be
with her. And when I danced with her, I had a good feeling
about myself. This had happened in a matter of a couple of
hours. How could I, as a fifteen year-old, be so sure and make
such a commitment?

Yvonne left the dance early with her girlfriend. I had her name.
Or at least I thought I did. She said her name is Yvonne: Yvonne
Polak. Now, was Polak her surname or was she telling me her
nationality? It took me a couple of months to figure that one out.
She did say she would come back to another Friday night social
when she could. This was the beginning of a love story that
continues to this day. As teenagers, we became the closest of
friends. That initial attraction is unexplainable, but it was the
force that allowed the bonding of friendship that grew into love.
My promise made at such an early age was about something of
which I knew little. The coming years would bring a better
understanding and fulfillment of that promise by the making of a
new promise. The promise to marry was replaced with the
promises to each other on our wedding day.

The New Testament brings a continuation to the story of God's
love. While the Old Testament was a message to the nation of
God's chosen people, the New Testament is a message to each
individual chosen by God. The promise of the New Testament is
the union of the individual with the community of God's chosen
people in His heavenly kingdom.

The new covenant is a restatement of Old Testament promises
based on new facts: the presence of God on earth in the person
of Jesus. The following table is how I see this New Testament
Covenant:

Jesus Brings Us a New Covenant

"This is my blood of the covenant, which is poured out for many for the forgiveness of sins." (Matthew 26:28)

New Testament Covenant		
Element	**Text**	**Meaning**
Promise	"Forgiveness of sins"	If we confess our sins, they will be forgiven (1 John 1:9)
Obligation	Serve others (Matthew 20:26-28)	We must love our neighbors as ourselves (Matthew 22:39). Humility, service and sacrifice are necessary.
Prophecy	The Spirit will tell you what is yet to come (John 16:13)	The Holy Spirit will be with us as Counselor forever (John 14:16). We are to go and make disciples of all nations (Matthew 28:19).

As in a will, where there is a covenant there must be a death to complete the promise. Jesus completes the promise for the forgiveness of sins. In this new covenant, we have the assurance of the promised eternal life. It is written in the blood of our Lord. "For this reason Christ is the mediator of a new covenant, that those who are called may receive the promised eternal inheritance—now that he has died as a ransom to set them free from the sins committed under the first covenant." (Hebrews 9:15)

Milestone #19

Know that your sins will be forgiven.

1. Jesus demonstrated the power to drive away evil spirits (Luke 4:31-37, 9:37-43). Why would this make the Sadducees and Pharisees angry? What does driving out evil spirits mean to you?

2. Do you hold a grudge against anyone? Do you know of someone that has wronged you, and you still are angry with them? Explain. Can you find it within yourself to forgive them? What are the barriers? What should you do, if anything, about this situation?

3. Do you feel someone is holding a grudge against you? Why? How do you feel about that? Do you feel you did something wrong? Do you feel you should be forgiven? What should you do about this situation?

4. Why is the forgiveness of sins so important? Do you feel you have sins that have not been forgiven? Why?

5. What action is required by the individual to receive the forgiveness of sins (1 John 1:9)? How do you perform this action? How do you feel others should perform this action?

6. Do you believe that Jesus has the power to forgive sins? Why? Do you believe the promise to forgive is made to you personally? Why, or why not?

Other New Testament Promises

After a couple of years of courting, Yvonne and I decided to get married. High school was behind us, I had a secure job, and we both felt we were ready to be on our own. After some serious discussions with our parents, we obtained their blessings.

That Saturday morning was a rainy, dreary day. It seemed from that day on all of our important events would occur on a day that had some rain. Perhaps it was to signify that the most happy of occasions would have some dark cloud, however small, associated with it. That certainly is what we have experienced over the years. In any event, it was a small wedding. Only the closest of family was present for the ceremony. The wedding took place in the cathedral in Baltimore. Being Lutheran at the time, I was not allowed to approach the altar any closer than the railing. Somehow this made me seem distant to the ceremony, even though Yvonne was by my side. I wanted to be closer to the altar, the image of God on earth.

Also, not being Catholic, I was required to attend six or seven sessions of indoctrination of the Roman Catholic faith to prepare for marrying into the faith. As it turned out I only attended one session. A young priest was assigned to me to give instructions. During the first session, I began to tell the priest what I knew about the Catholic faith and how I felt it compared to the Lutheran faith. Soon the young priest was asking me questions. He was interested in my view of the differences and my reasoning for being Lutheran. The Monsignor entered the room and listened to our conversation for a while. Then the Monsignor brought the session to a close and asked to see me privately. He then suggested that I need not return for the remaining sessions and that he was authorizing the marriage. I never was quite sure of why he did this. So I found myself at the cathedral making a life-long commitment.

Yvonne and I were but teenagers, and many said we were too young
to marry. But we were older than our years. Both of us had taken
on significant responsibilities at home. We were the oldest child in
each of our families. Siblings and cousins had been looking up to
us; our parents had been depending on us. Now we were confident
in our capability to be on our own. Now we were making new
promises to each other. Promises that would carry us through a
lifetime of love and devotion to each other.

"I, William Johnson, take thee, Yvonne Polak, to my wedded
wife, to have and to hold from this day forward, for better for
worse, for richer for poorer, in sickness and in health, to love and
to cherish, till death us do part, according to God's holy ordi-
nance; and thereto I plight thee my troth."

Needless to say, I wasn't sure what all of that meant. At the
time, I didn't even know what the words, "I plight thee my troth"
referred to. It was much later that I learned it meant to pledge
fidelity. Troth is a variant of truth. I pledged to be faithful and
true to Yvonne. That has been the easy part of my new promises.
Yvonne made it easy for me to be always faithful to her. There
was never any desire to do otherwise. Understanding "for
worse", "for poorer" and "in sickness" became continuing
lessons for me as the years went on. For these are the conditions
that Yvonne had to deal with in putting up with me. Fortunately,
Yvonne made the same promises to me.

Recently, our children gave us a surprise fortieth anniversary
party. I believe it is the only real surprise party I ever had. We
entered the party room at one of our favorite restaurants and
were greeted by family and friends. Neither Yvonne nor I were
dressed for a party, so we were (at least Yvonne was) a little
uneasy about our appearance. It was a grand time though. The
children had conspired to put together a display of those early
years. The wedding pictures and high school yearbook brought
back the feelings of those teenage years. And now, to look
around and see our family and friends, and to remember those

that could not be there.... It was a happy, emotional experience for me.

That very young couple in the wedding picture could not possibly be us. Surely, forty years could not have gone by so quickly. Yet the evidence is there in our children and grandchildren. I thought back to those promises made so long ago. My heart gave a silent thanks to God for the blessings that resulted from holding to the promises that Yvonne and I had made to each other. I am still learning the true meaning of those promises. It is a learning experience that I enjoy sharing with Yvonne.

The New Testament brings us many new promises. To me, I see it as a building on the promises of the Old Testament. They do not replace the old promises, but rather refine them and make them applicable to each individual. An individual's obligation to each of the New Testament promises is the same: To be obedient to God's word and believe in Jesus Christ.

These promises are made to each of us. Some are more relevant depending on the immediate circumstances. In each one of them, I have found meaning at one time or another. They reach out to all believers: the afflicted, the tempted, the penitent, the obedient, the seekers, the humble, the generous, the religious workers. In every situation in my life, I find a reassuring promise that brings hope into my thoughts. In turn, these hopeful thoughts bring a more righteous attitude to my actions. The promises of what is to be seems to make the obstacles of today less burdensome.

The following table reflects a selection of ten promises that are particularly meaningful to me. There are many more available to the searching heart. In the search to find a promise that is special to the individual, the individual is brought closer to God.

Promises to the Individual

"For no matter how many promises God has made, they are 'Yes' in Christ. And so through him the 'Amen' is spoken by us to the glory of God." (2 Corinthians 1:20)

Subject	Reference	Text
Obedience	John 14:23	"Jesus replied, 'If anyone loves me, he will obey my teaching. My Father will love him, and we will come to him and make our home with him.'"
The devil	James 4:7	"Submit yourselves, then, to God. Resist the devil, and he will flee from you."
Temptation	1 Corinthians 10:13	"No temptation has seized you except what is common to man. And God is faithful; he will not let you be tempted beyond what you can bear. But when you are tempted, he will also provide a way out so that you can stand up under it."
Seeking	Luke 11:9	"So I say to you: Ask and it will be given to you; seek and you will find; knock and the door will be opened to you."
Affliction	Romans 8:28	"And we know that in all things God works for the good of those who love him, who have been called according to his purpose."
Believing	Mark 11:24	"Therefore I tell you, whatever you ask for in prayer, believe that you have received it, and it will be yours."
Generosity	Luke 6:38	"Give, and it will be given to you. A good measure, pressed down, shaken together and running over, will be poured into your lap. For with the measure you use, it will be measured to you."
Prayer	John 14:13	"And I will do whatever you ask in my name, so that the Son may bring glory to the Father."
Holy Spirit	John 14:16	"And I will ask the Father, and he will give you another Counselor to be with you forever--"
Eternal Life	1 John 2:25	"And this is what he promised us -- even eternal life."

It is comforting to me to know that, in each and every crisis in my life, there is reason to hope. I can identify to a very specific promise that is made to me by God, through Jesus. I am not alone, for God has anticipated my situation and has provided for it. In any trial and tribulation, He will make a way out so that I can bear up under the strain of this life. And as I serve others, to His glory, He will recognize that and reward the humble and generous heart.

Milestone #20

Believe in the fulfillment of promises made to you by Jesus.

1. What is the difference, if any, between the Old Testament promises of God and the New Testament promises of Jesus? Are the New Testament promises in harmony with the Old Testament promises? Explain.

2. Do you believe the promises made by Jesus apply to you personally? Why, or why not?

3. Read 2 Peter 1:3-4. What promise from Jesus is most important to you? Why? When and how do you feel that promise will be fulfilled?

4. What is required from the individual to receive the benefits of the New Testament promises? Are you fulfilling your obligation? Why, or why not?

5. Do others support you in your promise to fulfill your obligations identified in question 4. above? How? Is support from others necessary? Why? Do you support others in their promises? How?

6. Participate in a prayer of thanksgiving to Jesus for the promises given to you and the hope for their fulfillment.

New Birth

Miraculous Births

When our granddaughter, Sarah Anne, was born two years ago, I considered it a miracle birth. Actually, I consider the creation of any new life a miracle, but this was an exceptional miracle. Our daughter, Stephanie, had a very difficult pregnancy, and this resulted in a premature birth. It was a life threatening situation for first, the mother-to-be, and then, the newborn infant.

Stephanie had a couple of stays in the hospital intensive care unit and a couple of visits home so Yvonne could care for her. On the last trip to the intensive care unit, Stephanie asked us to pray for her. We spent the whole night praying and asking for Jesus' healing presence to be with our daughter and soon-to-be-born granddaughter. It was a constant worry. When Sarah Anne was born she spent the first week in an incubator and an additional week in the hospital before she was allowed to go home. But, by the grace of God, both are doing well now. Sarah Anne's interest in Jesus, in going to church and in praying may be a result of the intense praying her grandparents did before she came into this world.

At the time Sarah Anne was born, I was out of town on a business trip. I got the call late on the evening of December 3, 1991 that Stephanie was being rushed to the hospital. Immediately, my prayers went out to Stephanie and the soon-to-be-born infant. Then I made reservations for the earliest available flight home, which was noon the next day. I was filled with anxiety. Yvonne was at home filled with the same anxiety. After a telephone conversation with Bruce, he decided to drive from Virginia to Pennsylvania to pick up Yvonne and then they would drive together to New Jersey to be with Stephanie. It was a long night for both of them. Bruce was there to comfort and support the family.

The morning that Sarah Anne was born my Bible reading contained the following passage: "Sons are a heritage from the Lord, children a reward from him. Like arrows in the hand of a warrior are the sons born in one's youth. Blessed is the man whose quiver is full of them. They will not be put to shame when they contend with their enemies in the gate." (Psalm 127:3-5) How proud I was of Bruce and his response, and how proud I was of Stephanie and her strength to survive the difficulty of the pregnancy. Surely I was blessed with such fine children.

Early afternoon of the next day, with little or no sleep, Bruce drove to Pennsylvania to meet my flight. We then drove back to New Jersey. I remember the first sight of my granddaughter. She was so small. I was very concerned about holding her. But I cradled her in my hand and silently thanked the Lord for this little miracle. Bruce was every bit the proud uncle and paced outside the windowed nursery, taking pictures and waving to his newborn niece. Of course, Yvonne played the role of the proud grandmother as she talked admiringly of her new granddaughter and cuddled her gently. The anxious night before had turned into a joyous day.

This wasn't the only difficulty our family experienced in bringing children into the world. Yvonne went through a trying miscarriage between the two boys, and later had the burden of delivering a still-birth child that had been very active during most of the pregnancy.

These experiences demonstrated just how fragile new birth can be. The full support of family and friends is required to get through the hurt. But the memory is always there. Tragic endings in childbirth can not be forgotten and happy endings will always be cherished.

The start of a new life, a new worldly being, is an important event. All participants look to the hope that is in the infant and wonder about the future. Each new life will make a difference, and everyone that touches the life of the child has the potential of directing what that difference will be. The miracle of birth is followed by the miracle of life itself.

The Bible contains stories of every aspect of life in this world. Within it are many new birth stories. Some of these reflect unusual and special conditions. The story of Jesus' birth is known throughout the world, and the special conditions of that birth reflect the miraculous intervention by God the Father. But that is not the only miraculous birth recorded in the Bible. Perhaps the special births were to have a special message for us. In these stories, one can find the hope for each new birth. In having that hope, one somehow feels better about their own future.

The following table presents the extra-ordinary, or miraculous, births that I noted:

Extra-Ordinary Births

"Then Esau looked up and saw the women and children. 'Who are these with you?' he asked. Jacob answered, 'They are the children God has graciously given your servant.'" (Genesis 33:5)

Reference	Mother	Child	Comments
Genesis 18:10-14 Genesis 21:1-3	Sarah	Isaac	Isaac became the father to Jacob, the founder of the nation of Israel.
Judges 13:2-3, 24	Wife of Manoah	Samson	Samson became the warrior-hero in the period of the judges that delivered the Israelites from the Philistines.
2 Kings 4:14-17	Shunammite Woman	Unnamed in text	At a young age, the child died and Elisha raised him from the dead because of the mother's faith.
Luke 1:13-16	Elizabeth	John	John became known as John the Baptist and was the messenger of the Lord.
Matthew 1:18-23 Luke 1:26-35	Mary	Jesus	Son of God, Lord and Savior of the chosen people.

I see in these stories a progression: The beginning of a great nation, the deliverance of that nation from the enemy, the foretelling of "the resurrection", the sending of a messenger to announce the Prince of Peace, and the deliverance of individuals from the evil one. Each of these special birth stories has great significance to me and reflect an order to God's plan for the salvation of each individual.

Milestone #21

Look for the miracle of creation in each new birth.

1. Do you know of an unusual or difficult birth? What made the event noteworthy? What impact did this have on the father and mother? The child? Others?

2. When you see an infant or small child, what thoughts come to mind about the child? About yourself? How do you feel being near an infant, particularly a close family member?

3. What are some of the qualities you best remember about your mother?

4. Read Matthew 1:18-25. Believing that Jesus was born of a virgin is critical to a full knowledge of who Jesus is. Why?

5. Read Luke 1:26-35. Have the Scriptures established that neither Joseph or any other man contributed to the conception of Jesus? Explain.

6. It is said that the greatest loss is the mother's loss of a child, yet there are so many incidents of infant death and child abuse reported. Why would a father or mother ever harm their own child? What is missing from the parents' life to cause them to do such acts? What can be done to help these troubled parents?

Baptism

I recall my baptism. My Mother invited the minister to our house to perform the ceremony. I was twelve years old, and I remember how excited my Mother was about the event. She made me wear my best Sunday outfit. Family members living in the area were invited over and she got a decorative glass bowl to hold the baptismal water. The ceremony passed quickly and I attached no particular importance to it, but I knew it was important to my Mother.

It was explained to me that this service was necessary to wash away my sins and allow me to receive the Holy Spirit. I heard the words, but I didn't feel any change take place. I wasn't even sure that I had any real sins that were bad enough to require being washed away. Although I didn't realize it at the time, I now know that a change did occur. At least the beginning of a change occurred. The Holy Spirit entered my being and is still making changes in my life to this very day.

Over the years, I have been elected Godparent to several children. I accepted that responsibility with every intent of nurturing the child's spiritual growth. It has only been in recent years that I truly understood that responsibility. I regret my neglect at fulfilling those responsibilities in the past. My resolve is to do all I can to fulfill them in the future.

Within the last two years, we have been blessed with two wonderful granddaughters. A few months after they were born, there was a Baptismal Service and Christening party for each of them. These events caused me to reflect on the meaning of baptism.

Our second granddaughter was born to Bruce and Kathy just a few months ago. As with our first granddaughter, I was out of town on a business trip. The delivery of this granddaughter, however, was basically on schedule and without the difficulty surrounding the arrival of our first granddaughter. Taylor came into this world as a radiant and beautiful child. Certainly a reflection of her loving parents. Yvonne and I anxiously awaited the weekend to make our visit to Virginia to see Taylor. She was all we expected. From the very beginning she has been a happy and content child.

The next few months passed ever so quickly. We only had a couple of visits with Taylor, and with each visit she was growing so much. Yet always she had that quick smile and the beautiful, radiant face. It is such a joy to see how Bruce and Kathy adore their new daughter. And now the baptismal day has arrived. The excitement of the day was magnified by the fact that Yvonne's niece was having her third child baptized at the same service as Taylor's. It was a day of double joy for all the family.

Michael and his family flew in from California, and for a very special weekend our entire family was together. These events bring such joy and happiness as we share with each other the fellowship and love of a closely bonded family.

Yvonne and I wrote a letter for each of our granddaughters and gave it to them on their special day. The following excerpts from those letters reflects the importance of their new life to us:

"Dear Sarah,

"...God looked down on us and saw suffering. He sent Jesus and asked that we have faith in His Son. For in that faith we will find hope and from that hope will come love. The more faith we have, the more hope there is within us. The more hope within us, the more love we share. The more love we share, the more our faith grows.

"It is in this we have the power of life...

"God looked down again and saw we still had sadness; and this did cause Him to mourn. He sent us then a miracle, the day

Sarah Anne was born. He sent us a happy, beautiful, loving child. A new life, a new beginning, a new hope, a new joy. Your life has already brought new meaning to those who love you. You see, with unobstructed vision, the love that surrounds you. And you have caused a light to pierce the darkness of our past. In that light, we see the hope that we have forgotten; in that light, we see the need to share our love; in that light, we find the fragments of our faith.

"God knew we needed you. Together we will live the life God has planned for us. Our love for you grows each day. May it become as boundless as God's love for us all."

"Dear Taylor,

"...The miracle of birth is the most precious of God's blessings. It is in each new life that God renews His promises of forgiveness, protection and mercy. And it is in each new life that an awareness of God is born rich in the hope of tomorrow.

"From the richness of God's grace you were sent to us that October evening. As a beautiful, healthy, radiant infant you brought to your parents, and to us, a fulfillment of great expectations. In the fragile life of that infant you bring much joy, love and hope. The love of those around you reflects from you and unites with the love of God that is within you to bring light and joy to all. In you, each of us have a new beginning.

"This day the Holy Spirit has united with the cleansing water of the baptismal fountain. With the anointing oil you were prepared to receive the Holy Spirit. Your very special parents, together with family and friends, have gathered to celebrate the Spirit that is now within you. Through the support of those with you this day, 'you have put on the new self, which is being renewed in the image of the Creator'. In that new self is the new hope of eternal life.

"God knew we needed you. He has given us the opportunity to share our love with a precious little girl. Our love for you grows each day...

"Being kept in Christ, we remain your loving Grandparents."

The message from this last letter was beautifully summarized when two-year old, Sarah Anne whispered to Yvonne at the close of the service, "Now Taylor has Baby Jesus in her heart."

The significant elements of the sacrament of baptism is the laying on of hands, the rejection of the devil, and the unity of the forgiveness of sins and regeneration. Water symbolizes the washing away of sins. Just as everyone is born with a nature of goodness, so they are born with the worldly nature of sin (original sin). The laying on of hands has had significance throughout history. It is a transference of power. The anointing of oil provides the medium to make reception of the Holy Spirit possible. For infants, the parents and godparents pronounce the rejection of the devil, made possible by the power of the presence of the Holy Spirit. Rejection of the devil allows for the Holy Spirit to fill the void and bring a new life; one not burdened with the sinful nature.

One may ask if baptism is really necessary. But in asking they fail to see the significance of all the elements required to bring the Holy Spirit into one's life. This is not symbolism. It is the workings of God.

Need for Baptism

"Jesus answered, 'I tell you the truth, no one can enter the kingdom of God unless he is born of water and the Spirit.'" (John 3:5)

	Old Testament	New Testament
Cleansing Commanded	"O Jerusalem, wash the evil from your heart and be saved. How long will you harbor wicked thoughts?" (Jeremiah 4:14)	"Come near to God and he will come near to you. Wash your hands, you sinners, and purify your hearts, you double-minded." (James 4:8)
Ceremonial Cleansing	"The person to be cleansed must wash his clothes, shave off all his hair and bathe with water; then he will be ceremonially clean." (Leviticus 14:8)	"They are only a matter of food and drink and various ceremonial washings -- external regulations applying until the time of the new order." (Hebrews 9:10)
Spiritual Cleansing	"I will sprinkle clean water on you, and you will be clean; I will cleanse you from all your impurities and from all your idols." (Ezekiel 36:25)	"How much more, then, will the blood of Christ, who through the eternal Spirit offered himself unblemished to God, cleanse our consciences from acts that lead to death, so that we may serve the living God!" (Hebrews 9:14)

It is easy to see how different the New Testament baptism is from the Old Testament baptism. Peter states it as follows: "God waited patiently in the days of Noah while the ark was being built. In it only a few people, eight in all, were saved through water, and this water symbolizes baptism that now saves you also — not the removal of dirt from the body but the pledge of a good conscience toward God. It saves you by the resurrection of Jesus Christ..." (1 Peter 3:20-21)

Milestone #22

Be born of the Spirit and cleansed
with water through baptism.

1. Why is it important to wash our hands before handling food, or eating, or putting in contact lens? Is this considered symbolic, or are there real health reasons for doing this?

2. Many people have claimed that the cleansing commands found in the Old Testament were made for sanitary reasons. What is your impression of the purpose for washing as stated in the Old Testament readings contained in the chart, Need for Baptism? (See also, Exodus 30:20, Leviticus 16:26-28, Ezekiel 36:25-26.)

3. What is the significance of the use of water in the baptismal ceremony?

4. Have you been baptized? Do you recall your baptism? What significance, if any, did your baptism have to you when the event took place? Now? If you don't recall your baptism, is it necessary to be baptized again? Why?

5. Do you feel everyone should be baptized? Why? When should they be baptized? Why? Who is empowered to baptize others? Why?

6. Baptism by water was done before the time of Jesus. John was baptizing with water before the ministry of Jesus. What is different about baptisms since the ministry of Jesus? How do you know you have been "born of the Spirit"?

The Redemptive Plan

Stephanie has had a difficult life since her teenage years. Many physical and emotional problems resulted in numerous hospital stays and treatment. It was difficult for those who loved her to determine the real nature and cause of the illness. As parents, we constantly sought those answers that were so elusive. Was it something genetic that we had missed in the adoption evaluations? Was there some mysterious, underlying sickness for which there wasn't a cure? Was it the result of our parental judgment and the environment we created for her?

From the very day we brought Stephanie home, she was treated as a small, porcelain, fragile doll by us and by her older brothers. Her petiteness and beauty have carried from childhood into womanhood. Her congeniality and child-like enthusiasm brings much joy to those in her company. But as a teenager she began a pattern of disobedience against us that started a gradual separation from us. The more disobedient she became, the more rules we put in place. The intent of these rules was to protect her from the world she was so anxious to experience.

She was intent to experience it all. How could she know how painful that would be? A rebellious teenager became a young woman with the same restless nature. After a short courtship that led to an early marriage, she experienced a disastrous honeymoon that doomed the relationship. Both her physical and emotional problems became increasingly evident. Without time for recovery from any of her illnesses, she entered into another relationship that led to her second marriage some two years later. Throughout this time, Stephanie seemed to separate herself from us more and more. We thought our love for her would be enough; it would overcome all.

This marriage, too, was a stormy relationship between Stephanie and her spouse. The illnesses continued and her general health condition was worsening. But then she gave birth to Sarah

Anne. During the pregnancy and the time following the birth, we noticed a definite change in Stephanie. She wanted us around her more and she called Yvonne every day just to talk about the events of the day. More than this, we saw a change in her attitude towards life in general. She wanted to attain spiritual growth. Then, one Saturday morning, we got a call from Stephanie's husband to come and get Stephanie and Sarah Anne because he couldn't deal with them anymore.

That ninety-mile drive to the New Jersey coast was an anxious one for us. We didn't really know what to expect, but we did know that our daughter and granddaughter needed us. That was nearly a year ago now; Stephanie and Sarah Anne are still with us. Stephanie is going through a very stormy and stressful separation. Her estranged husband does not understand, nor is he willing to participate in, the spiritual growth that Stephanie is now enjoying. The change in Stephanie has been truly remarkable. Her health condition has stabilized and she looks and acts like her "old self".

Since the adoption, Stephanie has always been, and always will be, our daughter. Her relationship with us will never change. For a period of time her choices brought about a separation in our fellowship. That fellowship has now been restored. That restoration was brought about in the birth of her daughter. Something has caused Stephanie to desire that fellowship with us. It was always there for her to have. Yvonne and I both prayed that since we didn't know what to do for Stephanie, we were turning her over completely to Jesus so that He may care for her. Jesus has brought her back to us and we are enjoying the completeness of the fellowship with her and Sarah Anne.

In looking back at our interaction with Stephanie, I see an outpouring of love. The trust given in that love was violated, whether unintentional or intentional. Loss of trust resulted in establishing rules of order, which in turn were twisted, turned and distorted to Stephanie's own liking. This resulted in a separation that we felt would never be overcome. Then Jesus interceded and reestablished the full fruits of the love we all once shared. It is not a plan that I could have devised, but it is a plan that brought wonderful results.

God has crafted a plan for us. It is one that assures our eternal life The plan is simple and it is always responsive to our failings. I see the plan as follows:

Stages in the History of Mankind

"The former regulation is set aside because it is weak (for the law made nothing perfect), and a better hope is introduced, by which we draw near to God." (Hebrews 7:18-19)

Condition	Type of Law	Comments
Innocent participation	Natural Law	Mankind lives in full harmony with all of creation.
Fall from grace	Disobedience	Choices toward self-reliance rather than trust in God's love
Compliance to priestly laws	Law of Justice	Obedience to commands to offset the temptations of original sin that distort the knowing of righteousness
Manipulation of the laws	Distortion	Interpreting the Mosaic laws of Sinai to satisfy one's desires
Established in Christ	Law of Love	Faith in Jesus and His atoning sacrifice for the sins of the world
Eternal peace	Law of the Spirit	Union with God

There is a progression that is obvious in this table. God's original Law of Love (Natural Law) is given to individuals. Worldly temptation brings about a separation from God. But God provides for a set of laws to guide a nation of His chosen. After time, these laws are redefined through self-interest interpretations. God then provides for a reestablishment of the Law of Love and confirms this with each individual through Christ. This then provides for the Law of the Spirit given to the community of saints.

Reconciliation, redemption, salvation and atonement are all terms we have heard many times. They all relate to the gift of God that brings everlasting life. Salvation generally relates to the education of mankind in the terms of the law, i.e., understanding righteousness. Reconciliation pertains to the renewed fellowship with God. Redemption is the plan that God put in place before the beginning of time to ensure a path for mankind to travel toward righteousness. For me atonement is better understood if shown as follows: AT—ONE—MENT. That is to say, at one with God, through Jesus Christ. It is the end result of the redemptive plan.

Atonement is possible only through faith. It is truly a gift of God. Many theories have been proposed over the centuries, but there is no absolute Theory of Atonement. Anselm of Canterbury, a medieval bishop, wrote a doctrine of atonement that makes a lot of sense to me. The following briefly states the essence of the elements of this doctrine. A Bible reference is given to reflect a specific passage that helped me in understanding the doctrine. This is not to imply that the reference is the biblical evidence supporting the element of the doctrine.

1. The honor of God is violated by human sin. For the sake of this honor it is necessary for God to respond in a negative manner. (Romans 3:23-26)

2. God has two possible ways to respond. Punishment, which results in eternal separation from God; or, satisfaction so that God may overlook the sins. Our merciful God decided to solve the problem through satisfaction. (Galations 3:13)

3. Humans are limited in their ability to fulfill this satisfaction and their guilt is infinite. Only God is able to give satisfaction to himself. (Titus 3:4-7)

4. However, it is the human, not God, who must give the satisfaction, since it is the human who sinned. Therefore, someone who is both human and God must do it, who as God can
   do it and as human must do it. Only a God-man is able to do
   this. (Romans 5:18)

5. This God-man could not make satisfaction through his deeds,
   since he had to do these anyhow out of full obedience to God.
   It is only through suffering that satisfaction can be made,
   since he did not have to suffer and was innocent. Christ's
   work is then voluntary to give satisfaction to God.
   (Hebrews 5:8-9)

6. Although human sin is infinite, this sacrifice, made by God
   himself, is also infinite. This makes it possible for God to
   give to Christ what he deserves. Christ asks of nothing for
   himself, but what he wants and needs are the humans that
   believe in Him and follow Him. (Ephesians 1:9-10)

Anselm's "credo ut intellium" is a statement that I can relate to.
I believe in order to understand. By believing, I find an increasing desire to search for understanding. By searching, I find an
increasing ability to understand. God is nurturing my growth.

Let us now look at how the doctrine of atonement is stated in the
Old Testament and the New Testament. From the Old Testament,
"Then he is to take the two goats and present them before the
Lord at the entrance of the Tent of Meeting. He is to cast lots for
the two goats — one lot for the Lord and the other for the
scapegoat. Aaron shall bring the goat whose lot falls to the Lord
and sacrifice it for a sin offering. But the goat chosen by lot as
the scapegoat shall be presented alive before the Lord to be used
for making atonement by sending it into the desert as a scapegoat." (Leviticus 16:7-10)

The bridge between the Old Testament atonement and the New
Testament atonement can be found in the following verse: "For

the life of a creature is in the blood, and I have given it to you to make atonement for yourselves on the altar; it is the blood that makes atonement for one's life." (Leviticus 17:11)

The New Testament doctrine states: "But God demonstrates His own love for us in this: While we were still sinners, Christ died for us. Since we have now been justified by His blood, how much more shall we be saved from God's wrath through Him! For if, when we were God's enemies, we were reconciled to Him through the death of His Son, how much more, having been reconciled, shall we be saved through His life! Not only is this so, but we also rejoice in God through our Lord Jesus Christ, through whom we have now received reconciliation." (Romans 5:8-11)

Milestone #23

Follow the Law of Love re-established in
Jesus and confirmed to individuals.

1. In your own words, describe how you believe God intended mankind to live on this earth? Would you define this as a natural law? If so, what label would you put on this law?

2. What does it mean to be redeemed? Explain in your own words Anselm's Doctrine of Atonement. What does atonement mean? How does it apply to you?

3. Read Psalm 31:5,130:7-8, Isaiah 43:1. Who is the author of redemption?

4. Read Hebrews 7:11-25. Why is Jesus compared to Melchizedek (see Genesis 14:18-24, Hebrews 7:1-10)? What change in the law do you think is referred to in Hebrews 7:12?

5. The Mosaic Law was delivered to reinstate the Hebrew nation after the fall from grace of all mankind. The Old Testament has more than 600 laws for the Hebrew nation. In Matthew 5:17, Jesus states that He has come to fulfill the law. What do you think His statement means?

6. Are you trusting Jesus for your fulfillment? Are you fulfilled? What areas in your life do you feel you need help to become fulfilled?

Born Again

In June 1988 Yvonne and I received an invitation to attend a dinner party. The red ink used to hand address the envelope and the red ink on the printed white invitation gave indication that this was not just an ordinary dinner party. Yvonne and I had no idea what to expect and timidly accepted the invitation. That dinner experience has become one of the most memorable events of our lives. As we entered the gates of the estate, we were directed to park on the lawn. There were already forty to fifty cars there before us. Casually, we followed others across the lawn to the back of the house. There were many tables set up and a couple of tents from which the buffet-style dinner would be served later in the evening. Formally dressed attendants with white gloves invited us over to a refreshments table to get a before-dinner drink. It was a surprise to find that the champagne type bottles really contained sparkling cider.

With filled glasses, Yvonne and I found our way to an empty table. Two additional couples joined us and then a third couple. We were speculating as to what to expect. It was announced later that due to the coolness of the evening there had not been the usual reception line where the hostess would have introduced herself and the special guests of the evening. The dinner and desserts were outstanding, but that is not what I particularly remember about the event.

One of my sports heroes, Ray Berry, was the guest speaker. At that time he was the head coach of the New England Patriots. I knew him better as the guru of the side-line pass from the glory days of the Baltimore Colts. But that night he quietly spoke of the meaning of receiving Jesus into your life. He spoke of a personal relationship with the Lord, and how there is an emptiness within us that can only be filled by Jesus. He further pointed out that logical acceptance of Jesus was not enough; you must willingly let go of everything else and allow Jesus to take control of your life.

Wow! That had quite an impact on me. It was then I realized that I was missing a personal relationship with Jesus. That evening I invited Jesus into my heart as a permanent guest. I had received a new awakening of my spirituality. It was as though it had gone into hibernation and had just been touched by the springtime sun. At the close of the program, I went to Ray to thank him and let him know that he gave me a memory that evening that is greater than any catch he ever made on a football field.

Yvonne had much the same reaction. She said she felt such a peacefulness come over her, and she suddenly knew that we would be led to solutions of the many problems that currently faced us. We sat and talked awhile, as the guests were leaving, to share with each other the wonderful gift we received that evening. There is no way for us to know how many of the other 400-plus guests might have been impacted the same way. For us, it was a personal experience brought on by the presence of Jesus at a Christian fellowship dinner. It was as though He soothingly held our hand to calm the turmoil within us. Without question, there was a dramatic change within us that night. A change that still is evolving six years later.

I have certainly heard the born again phrase before. Until that time, "born again Christian" had the stigma of being a fanatical, evangelical-type Christian. I always associated it with revival meetings and faith healings. Now I have a new perspective. I see born again as being a process of the Holy Spirit working within you. The first acceptance of the Holy Spirit at baptism gives it the opportunity to work within you. However, it takes some effort on the individual's part to nurture the growth and keep it active. As the individual reaches out to the Holy Spirit for growth, the growth is given and new opportunities for growth are put in its place.

The born again experience happens at baptism. But that doesn't mean that one cannot experience an event that is so filled with emotion and awe it changes one's life. It may be the result of a conversion to Christianity, or a touching act of human kindness, or a sense of sudden intervention by God. Label these as reborn experiences if you like. Then I submit that you may have more than one, indeed, possibly many, such experiences. They are all meaningful milestones in your progress along the path of spiritual growth.

The following table reflects the meaning of new birth as it pertains to the Christian.

New Birth for the Christian

"In reply Jesus declared, 'I tell you the truth, no one can see the kingdom of God unless he is born again.'" (John 3:3)

Element	Action	Result
The Word	"For you have been born again, not of perishable seed, but of imperishable, through the living and enduring word of God." (1 Peter 1:23)	"...put on the new self, which is being renewed in knowledge in the image of the Creator." (Colossians 3:10)
The heart	"I will give you a new heart and put a new spirit in you; I will remove from you your heart of stone and give you a heart of flesh." (Ezekiel 36:26)	"Therefore we do not lose heart. Though outwardly we are wasting away," (2 Corintians 4:16)
God's mercy	"...revive us, and we will call on your name." (Psalm 80:18)	"He saved us, not because of righteous things we had done, but because of his mercy. He saved us through the washing of rebirth and renewal by the Holy Spirit." (Titus 3:5)
God's will	"Repent, then, and turn to God, so that your sins may be wiped out, that times of refreshing may come from the Lord." (Acts 3:19)	"Do not conform to the pattern of this world, but be transformed by the renewing of your mind. Then you will be able to test and approve what God's will is -- his good, pleasing and perfect will." (Romans 12:2)
Childlike	"And He said, 'I tell you the truth, unless you change and become like little children, you will never enter the kingdom of heaven.'" (Matthew 18:3)	"Therefore, if anyone is in Christ, he is a new creation; the old has gone, the new has come!" (2 Corinthians 5:17)

God continues to reveal Himself to us in doses that we can absorb. He provides the opportunity, but it requires action on our part to grow. Sometimes the growth comes in spurts and often it is a slow, ever advancing process. It is up to each individual to participate in this growth to gain the fruits of the new birth. Be born again, and again, and again. But understand, after the baptism, each rebirth is but a spurt in your spiritual growth. A milestone along the journey toward the truth.

Milestone #24

Experience the rebirth of your spiritual growth.

1. What do you believe it means to be "born again"? Is this an unusual, evangelical experience? Explain.

2. Read John 3:1-13. Who was Nicodemus? Why do you think he came at night to talk with Jesus? What primary message was Jesus trying to give to Nicodemus? Do you think Nicodemus got the message (see John 7:50-52, 19:38-42)?

3. What do you believe having a personal relationship with Jesus means? Do you have that relationship? If so, how did you establish it? If not, how can you obtain it?

4. How would you explain childlike as stated in Matthew 18:3? What change would you have to make to become childlike?

5. Read John 1:10-13. How does one become a child of God? Who determines that an individual is a child of God?

6. Read 1 John 5:1-5. What is the evidence that an individual has new birth?

Preparation

Preparing to Pray

As a young adult I prayed often. Yvonne and I prayed together most every night. Things were going well for us. Then somewhere along the way, the prayers became less frequent, and eventually stopped altogether. Looking back, it seems that I had become completely self-reliant. Anything that I set my mind to do was accomplished. But I had ignored my dependence on God.

Well, the tide turned. I experienced unexpected career changes, health problems, financial hardships and family tragedies. My life was in turmoil. It was as though my life and emotions were on a roller coaster ride. At the bottom of each dip on this ride, I prayed with conviction. You know the type of praying I'm talking about. I prayed until I was sweating — not drops of blood, but certainly under strain. The prayers stopped as I came up from the dip, and I returned to my self-reliance as I got to the top of each cycle. I would pat myself on the back and say, "You really pulled yourself out of that situation." But the downward cycles were coming more frequently and each dip got deeper.

After a dozen or so years on that roller coaster ride, I came to the realization that I needed to establish a personal relationship with Jesus and talk to God more. I knew that prayer is the golden key that unlocks the storehouses of God's grace and love, but I forgot how to pray. The retraining in prayer was just a matter of following what I call the Ten Steps to Prayer. The following table provides the listing of these steps and the biblical reference for them:

Ten Steps to Prayer

Preparation Step	Reference	Comment
1. Read the Bible	Dt. 17:19	Daily reading of the Word will teach reverence and obedience to God.
2. Repeat a known prayer	Mt. 6:9-13	Praying aloud the Lord's Prayer will help to start the talk with God.
3. Express adoration	Mark 12:30	Begin by addressing God as Father, Lord or Friend for He is all of these.
4. Use your own words; be brief	Ecc. 5:1-3 Mt. 6:5-7	Say what needs to be said in a language that is comfortable.
5. Give thanks	1 Th. 5:18	There is something to be thankful for each and every day. All is from God.
6. Offer petitions; yourself and others	Phil. 4:6	In doing so be unselfish, willing to forgive and have a clean heart.
7. Confess wrongdoing	Psalm 66:18	Agree with God all wrong thoughts, desires and actions you have had.
8. Be persistent	1 Th. 5:17	God's time is not our time. Pray repeatedly and continually.
9. Pray in Jesus' name	Jn. 16:23-24	This reflects our personal relationship with Jesus.
10. Have faith	James 1:6 Mt. 21:22	We must have faith in Christ, in our redemption, and in the purpose of our prayer.

These ten steps have shown me that bad habits are overcome by prayer; evil thoughts and tendencies are rooted out by prayer; dark hours are made light by prayer. Prayer brings victory over life's difficulties, temptations and trials. Prayer is a powerful influence on how we live our life. The dictionary gives us a cut and dry definition of prayer as a solemn address to a supreme being. But prayer is more than this. It is a communion, the pouring out of the whole soul to God.

We are to pray in the Spirit and pray for others as Paul advises the Ephesians (6:18), "And pray in the Spirit on all occasions with all kinds of prayers and requests. With this in mind, be alert and always keep on praying for all the saints." In praying to the Spirit, the Spirit will intercede for us (Romans 8:26-27), "In the same way, the Spirit helps us in our weakness. We do not know what we ought to pray, but the Spirit himself intercedes for us with groans that words cannot express. And he who searches our hearts knows the mind of the Spirit, because the Spirit intercedes for the saints in accordance with God's will."

And Jesus tells us that our prayers will be answered (Mark 11:24), "Therefore, I tell you whatever you ask for in prayer, believe that you have received it, and it will be yours." An important element of prayer is persistence. For Jesus says (Luke 11:9), "Ask and it will be given to you; seek and you will find; knock and the door will be opened to you." What I see in this statement is that we are to keep asking, seeking, knocking. Then in God's time, He will respond.

Milestone #25

Learn to communicate with the Lord.

1. Is there any prayer that you have prayed, or read, or heard, that stands out in your memory? Why did this prayer stand out? Was it the event, or the words of the prayer? What feeling did you have during the praying, reading, or hearing of this prayer?

2. Do you ever pray to God? What is the purpose of your prayers? Do you believe all, or some, of your prayers are answered? Explain.

3. Do you feel comfortable praying? Why, or why not?

4. Do you use memorized prayers as your form of praying, such as, the Lord's Prayer, bedtime prayers, grace at meals? Where did you learn these prayers? Are memorized prayers your only type of prayers? If so, are there other prayer forms you should be using? Explain. If not, what other prayer forms do you use? Why do you use these forms of prayer?

5. Do you believe it is possible to concentrate enough on the prayer to put aside all other thoughts? Have you experienced that? If you did, was that a particularly memorable prayer? Should there be a time during your prayer that is silent of your words or thoughts? Why?

6. Do you believe the Lord communicates to individuals through their prayers? Explain. Do you believe the Lord has communicated with you through your prayers? Share that experience with others. Is this the only possible way the Lord communicates with you? Discuss.

Conditioning for Prayer

It has now been more than six years since I got back into a regular routine of prayer. Even after following the ten steps to prayer, I was not satisfied with my communication to God. I didn't feel the open, two-way dialogue that I knew was possible. For it to work for me, I had to give my prayer routine more structure. I began by setting aside time each day to concentrate on my talk to God. Being a morning person, I decided to spend the first 30 to 45 minutes in this effort. In addition to Bible reading and prayer meditation, I began what I call a Christian journal. Each day I enter my thoughts, questions, praise, prayer requests, verses that may have special meaning to me, and any interpretative meaning I may gather from my readings. Following is the first few sentences of my first journal entry:

> "The purpose of this log is to provide a formalized and disciplined communication with my God. An individual's faith is a very personal matter. Personal in that each person recognizes the presence of God through their own unique experiences and perceptions of those experiences.

> "This log is to be my personal reminder of the workings of God and my response to His will. I ask now that God provide me with the inspiration and awareness to record those threads of faith, hope and love that He weaves into the fabric of my faith. My private and personal prayers I pray to my God in secret as He has instructed me (Matthew 6:6): 'When you pray, go into your room, close the door and pray to your Father, who is unseen. Then your Father, who sees what is done is secret, will reward you.'"

My daily routine works for me; it wouldn't necessarily work for everyone else. Also, I don't want to leave the impression that this is the only time I pray. I converse with God often during the day, in less formalized manner. A benefit I get from my journal is that I can go back to see how often my prayers have been answered. Another benefit is that I can see if any changes occur in my communication with God. I can tell you that there has been, and continues to be, a change in my prayers. In the early journal entries, my prayers sounded something like, "Listen up Lord, this is how I want You to help me today!" More recently, the prayers are, "Lord, here I am. Let Your will direct me this day."

Over the years I came to understand the conditioning that is required for more meaningful prayers. This conditioning is a continuing process that nurtures the spiritual growth in individuals. I see the conditioning for prayer as follows:

Be right with yourself to get right with God

Condition	Reference	Text
Precursor to temptation	Matthew 26:41	"Watch and pray that you will not fall into temptation. The spirit is willing, but the body is weak."
Reverence	John 9:31	"We know that God does not listen to sinners. He listens to the godly man who does his will."
Mutual communication	John 15:7	"If you remain in me and my words remain in you, ask whatever you wish, and it will be given you."
Obedience	1 John 3:21-22	"If our hearts do not condemn us, we have confidence before God and receive from him anything we ask, because we obey his commands and do what pleases him."
Character of Christ	John 14:12-13	"Anyone who has faith in me will do what I have been doing.....And I will do whatever you ask in my name, so that the Son may bring glory to the Father."
Will of God	1 John 5:14	"This is the assurance we have in approaching God; that if we ask anything according to his will, he hears us."
In Jesus' name	Hebrews 4:14-15	"Therefore, since we have a great priest who has gone through the heavens, Jesus the Son of God, let us hold firmly to the faith we profess. For we do not have a high priest who is unable to sympathize with our weaknesses, but we have one who has been tempted in every way, just as we are -- yet was without sin."

The key conditioning factor is establishing the personal relationship with Jesus. He is at the door, knocking (Revelations 3:20). All we have to do is open the door and let Him in. No one gets to the Father, but through Jesus (John 14:6).

Milestone #26

Develop a daily habit of prayer.

1. How often do you pray? What is the environment in which you pray? Do you do any preparation for praying? If so, describe.

2. Read Hebrews 4:14-16, James 1:2-6, I Samuel 12:23. What do these verses say about prayer? How does that apply to you?

3. Is there a difference between praying and being prayerful? Explain. Do you know anyone that you describe as being prayerful? What are the significant traits that led you to identify the individual as being prayerful?

4. Following are times when you may have prayed or seen others pray. On a scale of 1 to 10 (10 = highest), rank your feeling of importance in praying at these times and explain your ranking:

    ____ At church service

    ____ Grace at meals, at home

    ____ Grace at meals, at public places

    ____ Before going to bed at night

    ____ Before beginning daily activities

    ____ Looking for a parking place

    ____ With a friend in a specific time of need

    ____ Whenever a need or praise of thanksgiving is thought of

5. How often do you really pray? How often do you believe you should pray? Is it better to have a specific time, or times, rather than spontaneous or ad hoc? Explain.

6. How can you improve your prayer habit? Do you believe you can be more prayerful? How?

Example of Prayer

It seems that everyone has been exposed to training in prayer. That training has generally come from prayer examples given by others. Tribal leaders through their chanting teach other tribal members how to chant for the intervention of some supreme being or to give thanksgiving for their provision. Shamans repeat a mantra to invoke a brief petition or sacred word and thereby teach their followers how to pray for special powers of self-control. Clergy provide direction to their congregations by praying, with them and for them, to God and provide many examples of prayer.

All of these examples reflect meaningful teachings that individuals can utilize in the development of their own prayer style and formula. Unfortunately for many, the style and formula become more important than the heart felt content of the prayer. Oh how easy it is to repeat words and not get involved with the deep feeling and sincere expression that is the very essence of prayerful communication.

Many times, in church, I have noticed people just mouthing their prayers. They were also busy looking randomly around, or fidgeting with something in their hand or purse, or interrupting the prayer to say something to someone next to them. This doesn't speak well of their attitude toward prayer. Of course, it doesn't speak well of my own attitude in prayer at the moment. But the point is that I sense so many people are saying prayers by rote; just repeating memorized verses. There seems to be no meaning in the communication, and little reverence to God.

On one occasion several years ago I was asked by a dear friend to give the blessing before the meal at the wedding reception of their son. While giving the blessing, I found it necessary to pause because a large group at the reception was busy talking loudly and seemed disruptive to what should have been a quiet and reverent moment. They obviously were not being courteous

to the others that wanted to share in the meaning of the invoca-
tion. I wondered at what example had been set in their life for
the offering of a prayer.

The home too offers the opportunity for obtaining examples of
prayer. Somewhere along the way everyone must have heard the
"Now I lay me down to sleep" evening prayer that parents pass
on to their children. Another example is the "God is great, God
is good" grace repeated over meals. Certainly, we taught our
children those prayers.

Recently, we visited Michael and his family. I was impressed
with the awareness that my grandson had for God and our
dependence on Him for he would often stop for a moment and
just say "Thank You, God..." for some little thing that would
otherwise have gone unnoticed by me. During our visit Yvonne
became ill and was not able to join the family at the dinner table.
Ryan volunteered to say the grace. Following the typical "God is
great...", he went on to say, "and please make my Gran Mommy
well because I have waited so long for her to come and I have so
much I want to do with her and to show her." He concluded with
a couple of other petitions that I do not recall. But that prayer
did impress me. I realized it was from the heart, without any
coaching. My grandson knew that the standard prayer was not
enough for the situation; it was but a springboard into the
expression of his concerns, needs and love. His example of
prayer is better than any I could give. It is but another incident
where my children and grandchildren are teaching me about the
meaning of life and how to live it properly. How quickly the role
of teacher changes to pupil and vice-versa.

A learned Pharisee named Nicodemus came to Jesus and said
(John 3:2), "Rabbi, we know you are a teacher who has come
from God." And surely, Jesus is our great and divine teacher.
He came to explain the ways of the Father so we could understand them; not only with words but by example. The Gospels
are filled with His teachings to His disciples, the multitudes and

individuals. The truth in these teachings has been validated time and time again through the ages. They applied to everyone those two thousand years ago; they apply to those on this earth today; they will be fresh to all who come after us. The books that have been written on the teachings of Jesus would fill a very large library. And when His teachings are written on the heart, they fill an eternity with love, peace and joy.

It is fitting then that we look to the divine teacher for instructions on how to pray. Jesus on a number of occasions would pray in public, but most often, He went off by Himself and prayed alone. It seems His preferred posture for prayer, when He was alone, was kneeling. While speaking to the multitudes in what is known as the Sermon on the Mount, Jesus gave instructions on how to pray. He, in fact, gave them an example of a proper prayer. A prayer that showed reverence to the Father and also addressed the basic needs of each of us. It is a prayer that can be repeated time and time again while still holding relevance to the moment.

Matthew records what Jesus teaches about how to pray. The following table presents the elements of the Lord's Prayer. The background text brings further biblical evidence of the need to include each prayer element and adds definition as to what the element may mean.

Jesus is the Great Teacher
Matthew 6:9-13

God's Glory:

Element of Prayer	Background
"hallowed be your name"	"This is because both of you broke faith with me.....and because you did not uphold my holiness....." (Dt. 32:51)
"your kingdom come"	"For you know very well that the day of the Lord will come like a thief in the night." (1 Th. 5:2)
"your will be done"	"My Father, if it is possible, may this cup be taken from me. Yet not as I will, but as you will." (Mt. 26:39)

Man's needs:

Element of Prayer	Background
"give us this day our daily bread"	"Therefore, do not worry about tomorrow, for tomorrow will worry about itself. Each day has enough trouble of its own." (Mt. 6:34)
"forgive us our debts"	"For if you forgive men when then sin against you, your heavenly Father will also forgive you. But if you do not forgive men their sins, your Father will not forgive your sins." (Mt. 6:14)
"lead us not into temptation"	"Do not store up for yourselves treasures on earth.....For where your treasure is, there your heart will also be." (Mt. 6:19-21)
"deliver us from evil"	"Turn from evil and do good.....The eyes of the Lord are on the righteous.....the face of the Lord is against those who do evil....." (Psalm 34:14-16)

It is important to note that prayer is not to inform God of our needs, but rather to have conscious communication with Him as His children. "Your Father knows what you need before you ask him." (Matthew 6:8)

Things do matter. They are to be enjoyed as gifts of a Father who loves us and cares for our needs. They are to inspire us and lift our heart to God. They are vehicles of our love to one another, expressing our personality and our love. It is the focus on the worldly things, the consuming desire for them, that turns our heart from God. For it is through things that the evil one finds his way into our life and fills us with greed and pride.

Milestone #27

Rely on the Lord for all things.

1. Are there symptoms of the self-made syndrome in life? Be open and honest with yourself and describe the symptoms.

2. Compare Luke 6:46-49 with Psalm 127:1-2. How does this correspond with your ideas of business? How does it correspond to your walk with the Lord?

3. What really motivates you? What are your objectives for business? Family? Faith?

4. Read Matthew 6:19-21. What are some of the "treasures in heaven" that you have waiting for you? How do you think you go about receiving these treasures?

5. What is the difference between needs and wants? Is it wrong to pray for our wants? Explain. Is it necessary to pray for our needs? Explain.

6. Read Matthew 6:33-34, 1 Peter 5:6-7. What does it mean to you to cast your cares upon the Lord? Do you feel you do this?

Jesus' Prayer for Us

A friend of mine was a successful businessman and he came to Christ about ten years ago. Then about four years ago, he gave up his business and became a missionary. He felt the calling to travel to the far ends of this world to bring the message of Jesus to others. On a recent visit of his back to the United States, we discussed his calling. He told me that he didn't understand the force behind his actions that led to the decision that changed his life. He went on to say, "I thought I knew about the power of prayer, and felt strongly that God was answering my prayers by directing me to the missionary work. It wasn't until I saw the fervor in the prayers of the Asians I was working with that I realized it wasn't my prayers that brought me there. It was their prayers. I was God's answer to their prayers. They taught me how to pray fervently. Oh, I still pray for myself, but not with the expectation that God will use me as His answer. For now I know that God can answer our prayers in ways that man can not imagine. Today my prayers are more persistent, sincere and emotional than ever before. I learned that by being a missionary."

God expects us to pray for ourselves, but He also expects us to pray for others. Our prayers surely reflect our love and concern for others. Have you ever asked anyone to pray for you? Has anyone ever asked you to pray for them? It is certainly natural to do so. Could it be that we sense someone else may be closer to God, and God will more likely hear that person? Well, God hears all of our prayers. I view it more as prayer being the training we require for the communication process we will have in eternal life. That process will include a dialogue with the Father and the content of that dialogue will be the care of all those we are concerned about and love, even those that we have left behind.

Jesus, as the great example, often prayed for Himself, for His disciples, for individuals, for the community of believers. The following table outlines one of His prayers for us:

The Great Intercessor
John 17

Element of Prayer	Verse	Text
Kept in the Father's name	11	"Holy Father, protect them by the power of your name"
Kept in safety	12	"I protected them and kept them safe by the name you gave me."
Kept in joyfulness	13	"I say these things while I am still in the world, so that they may have the full measure of my joy within them."
Kept in purity	15	"My prayer is not that you take them out of the world but that you protect them from the evil one."
Kept separated	16	"They are not of this world, even as I am not of it."
Kept in sanctification	17	"Sanctify them by the truth; your word is truth."
Kept in active service	18	"As you sent me into the world, I have sent them into the world."
Kept in perfect unity	21	"I pray also for those who will believe in me.....that all of them may be one."
Kept for the coming glory	24	"Father, I want those you have given to me to be with me where I am, and to see my glory"

It should be understood that this prayer is for all believers: "This prayer is not for them alone. I pray also for those who believe in me through the message." (John 17:20)

Milestone #28

Pray for others and have others pray for you.

1. Have you ever prayed for anyone else? Have you ever asked anyone to pray for you? Why would you ask someone to pray for you?

2. Should you wait for others to ask before you pray for them? How do you feel about praying for someone else? Do you feel your prayer will have more, the same, or less impact that the prayer of the person for whom you are praying? Explain.

3. Read Mark 11:24-25. What is Jesus' teachings about prayer in these verses? What does He say about praying for others?

4. Read John 17:1-5. Who is Jesus praying for in these verses? What is Jesus praying for? What does that mean to you?

5. Read John 17:6-19. Who is Jesus specifically praying for in these verses? Describe in your own words what Jesus is praying for. Are there any lessons learned about praying that you see in this? Explain. Read John 17:20-26. Who is Jesus praying for in these verses? Does His prayer apply to you? How?

6. Take five minutes, or more, to pray aloud asking God to be glorified and honored through your business, family, community and to show you how to better accomplish that.

Life Forces

Shekinah Glory

My Father and I were feeling so helpless. Something was happening to Mother. Symptoms of physical illness and behavior changes were taking place. Doctors did not know the cause, and we certainly didn't understand the problems. Then after another extended stay in the hospital, an intern suggested the possibility of a brain tumor. While this seemed to be a long shot, it was decided to perform surgery and evaluate the problem.

As so often has been the case over the past forty years, I was out of town on a business trip. Yvonne called to say that emergency surgery was scheduled for that day and I should be home when the results were made known. Immediately, I made arrangements to catch the very next flight home and arrived late that night.

It was too late. Mom died on the operating table. A very large tumor was discovered. The diagnosis was that it was a unique condition and the doctors didn't know much about it; only that it was rare and generally occurred in women at a fairly early age. Mom was only 38 years old. She did get to be with her first grandchild, Bruce, but had little opportunity to see her second, Michael, who was but an infant.

Oh how I mourned the loss. She was such a happy and vivacious woman. Only a few years before, she had taken up oil painting as a hobby and was creating some very good work. She was the motivating force holding our family together. Now she wouldn't have the opportunity to see her daughter marry and begin raising a family. Frequently, I would think about all that she was missing and how much I truly missed her. Dad's grief was even greater. He would just sit in a chair and stare out the window. Each day he would visit the cemetery and sit beside the gravesite and talk with Mom. I didn't know what he was thinking or saying. He was a private person, and this was especially a private matter between him and Mom.

For six months I continued to dwell on the loss and had recurring dreams of Mom. One particular night, again out of town, I was awakened from a deep sleep. It took a few seconds to orient myself in the hotel room. Then at the foot of my bed, the darkness changed to a brilliantly glowing light. Within that light, there was the image of a woman clothed in a long robe. I knew it was Mother. I really do not remember a word spoken to me or a response from me. Yet we were communicating. The message to me was that Mom was happy were she was. She was in an indescribable environment of joy and peace and beauty. I was not to worry about her nor feel guilty about all the things I thought I should have done for her. She knew of my love and I was always to remember her love for me.

Was it just a dream? Possibly, but unlike any other I ever had before or since. Was it just imagined images from my sub-conscious mind? I doubt it. Was it in fact reality? To me it was as real as reality can be for me. I do know my guilt-filled recurring dreams stopped that night. The daily wanderings of my mind about what should have been and what could have been concerning Mother stopped also. That night I experienced a reconciliation within myself and with Mother This is an event that I have not shared with anyone else over these many years, except for Yvonne. I will always remember the magnificent glowing image at the foot of my bed in some hotel room in the mid-west.

I think about that event whenever I read the Bible passages pertaining God's presence here on earth. Radiance emanating from God is a bright light. Light can be either source light or reflective light. For instance, the sun is source light and the moon has reflective light. God is a source light, referred to as the Shekinah Glory. There is much more to source light than just the shining. There is warmth and comfort, and more importantly, our response to it.

For the Jewish nation, God was present to guide them through the forty years of wanderings. God appeared as a pillar of cloud by day and a pillar of fire by night. The pillar of cloud went before them and led them on their journey. It provided shade from the intense heat of the desert sun; it stood between them and their enemies and protected them. As a pillar of fire, it provided light at night so they could travel by day or night. God was enthroned above the Ark of the Covenant and resided in the Tent of the Testimony in the Tabernacle, and later in the Holy of Holies in the Temple. No one could enter when God was present.

When God appeared to Moses on Mount Sinai, Moses had to hide from His presence and not look upon Him. Yet just being in His presence, Moses face had a reflective radiance that had to be veiled so that others could look at him. At Jesus' transfiguration, the witnessing disciples had to hide themselves from the radiance of God's presence.

Following is a table of the significant references to God's radiance:

The Presence of God

"An angel of the Lord appeared to them, and the glory of the Lord shone around them, and they were terrified." (Luke 2:9)

Event	Reference	Text
Giving of the law	Exodus 24:17-18	To the Israelites the glory of the Lord looked like a consuming fire on top of the mountain. Then Moses entered the cloud as he went on up the mountain. And he stayed on the mountain forty days and forty nights.
Reflective radiance	Exodus 34:29-30	When Moses came down from Mount Sinai with the two tablets of the Testimony in his hands, he was not aware that his face was radiant because he had spoken with the Lord. When Aaron and all the Israelites saw Moses, his face was radiant, and they were afraid to come near him.
God enthroned	Leviticus 16:2	The Lord said to Moses, "Tell your brother Aaron not to come whenever he chooses into the Most Holy Place behind the curtain in front of the atonement cover on the ark, or else he will die, because I appear in the cloud over the atonement cover."
Pillar of cloud & fire	Exodus 13:21-22	By day the Lord went ahead of them in a pillar of cloud to guide them on their way and be night in a pillar of fire to give them light, so that they could travel by day or night. Neither the pillar of cloud by day nor the pillar of fire by night left its place in front of the people.
Trans-figuration	Matthew 17:1-2	After six days Jesus took with him Peter, James and John the brother of James, and led them up a high mountain by themselves. There he was transfigured before them. His face shone like the sun, and his clothes became as white as the light.
Unveiled glory	2 Corinthians 3:18	And we, who with unveiled faces all reflect the Lord's glory, are being transformed into his likeness with ever-increasing glory, which comes from the Lord, who is the Spirit.
The New Jerusalem	Revelations 21:23	The city does not need the sun or the moon to shine on it, for the glory of God gives it light, and the Lamb is its lamp.

The reflected radiance in Moses' face was so brilliant that he had to wear a veil so that others may look upon him. The Temple had a very heavy veil before the Holy of Holies to protect the people from the light of God as He came before them. They were not ready to be in His presence. At Jesus' transfiguration, the disciples could not look upon Him. They, too, were not ready to see the Light. At Jesus' death on the cross, the veil before the Holy of Holies was torn in two. Possibly this is what Ezekiel was referring to when nearly six hundred years before he proclaimed, "I will tear off your veils and save my people from your hands, and they will no longer fall prey to your power. Then you will know that I am the Lord." (Ezekiel 13:21)

Through Jesus we can come before the Light. Moses was veiled, but we are unveiled. Jesus has prepared the way for us. We can reflect God's light for all to see. And then, in the New Jerusalem, we will be in union and forever be comforted by the source light of His being.

Milestone #29

Reflect God's light, unveiled, to bring glory to His name.

1. Read Matthew 17:1-9. Moses and Elijah appear with Jesus at the transfiguration. Why do you think they appear with Jesus (see Matthew 5:17)? What do you think Moses represents? Elijah? What is the significance of Jesus being alone when the Disciples look again? Discuss the implication of Peter's reaction. What instruction is Peter given?

2. What is the significance of the curtain in the temple being torn in two (Matthew 27:50-51)? Does this have any relevance to you? Explain.

3. Can you look directly at the sun? Why not? If you cannot look directly at the sun, how do you know it is there? What evidence do you rely on?

4. The moon gives light at night. Describe the light from the moon. What is the source of that light? Does this light have the same attributes of sun light? Explain.

5. What does it mean to you to reflect God's light? How can you do this?

6. How can you bring further glory to God's name? At home? At work? In the community?

Power

"As I write this, my weapons of war are ready. The enemy is defined. The mission is set. The planning is over. What remains before us is the completion of the task, the liberation of a nation, the destruction of a Godless nation who holds the world hostage.

"In a few days the lines which hold this implement of my President's will, will be untied and we shall speed to our task. The possibilities of my actions in the forthcoming weeks leave me both anxious and uneasy. We have worked hard making the ship capable of performing her designated mission. The C.O. is looking to me more each day in the employment of our new weapons. I am proud of my men.

"When we put to sea, we will be the most capable weapons platform ever brought against this nation. My prayers are that the war is over before we are needed. If not, we are ready. We shall not fail.

"…I love you dearly and keep in my heart our memories and our dreams of the future. Until then my friend, keep me close as I do you…Your son, Michael."

Operation Desert Storm was a brief military encounter in the early days of 1991. As the Weapons Officer of a "boomer" type, nuclear submarine, Michael began to think on the terrible responsibility of the job before him. He realized that the control of all this power brought with it certain responsibilities. Weeks before deploying into combat readiness, he had to adjust from the "war games" attitude to the reality of a true to life conflict.

The need to use the awesome power of those nuclear weapons never occurred. After the conflict, Michael stated that he had to deal with the awareness that the release of any one of the weapons would have resulted in the destruction of human life. Many unsuspecting and innocent people were in the shadow of doom. The responsibility of holding the lives of so many people in his hands suddenly weighed heavily on him. Yet the need to stop the oppression was there. The years of training and preparation had brought him to the brink of wielding mighty power. He knew that the men under his command depended on him; the Commanding Officer depended on him; the men and women on the front line of the conflict depended on him.

The question arose within his heart of the moral justice in the release of such power. He had no answer for that, but he knew he would not disappoint all those depending on him to perform his duty. The experience brought new meaning to Michael on service to others. With much deep thought, soul searching and prayer, he vowed that his future service to his country would in some way be linked to peaceful service that benefited mankind. His unique training and preparation will be used in more peaceful endeavors.

Mankind has the capability of destroying itself with the power harnessed through atomic research. Even this awesome power is insignificant to the power that comes from God. The Bible brings us two views of this power. The Old Testament view is one of a mighty force from God, while the New Testament is more of a gentle confidence within us directed by the Holy Spirit.

Power of the Old Testament

"He rules forever by his power, his eyes watch the nations -- let not the rebellious rise up against him. Selah." (Psalm 66:7)

Power Within	Reference	Text
God	Exodus 9:16	But I have raised you up for this very purpose, that I might show you my power and that my name might be proclaimed in all the earth.
70 Elders	Numbers 11:25	Then the Lord came down in the cloud and spoke with him, and he took of the Spirit that was on him and put the Spirit on the seventy elders. When the Spirit rested on them, they prophesied, but they did not do so again.
Othniel	Judges 3:10	The Spirit of the Lord came upon him, so that he became Israel's judge and went to war.
Gideon	Judges 6:34	Then the Spirit of the Lord came upon Gideon, and he blew a trumpet, summoning the Abiezrites to follow him.
Samson	Judges 14:6	The Spirit of the Lord came upon him in power so that he tore the lion apart with his bare hands as he might have torn a young goat.
Saul	1 Samuel 10:10	When they arrived at Gibeah, a procession of prophets met him; the Spirit of God came upon him in power, and he joined in their prophesying.
David	1 Samuel 16:13	So Samuel took the horn of oil and anointed him in the presence of his brothers, and from that day on the Spirit of the Lord came upon David in power.

God's awesome power was displayed in His protection of the Jewish nation. First in the escape from Egypt, then in the guidance across the wilderness, then in the defeat of the opposing nations as they settled in the land of the Canaanites. With the judges and kings the Spirit was sent in power to conquer rivals. But always the power was the direct action of God as a show of force to stop the threat to His chosen people.

Power in the New Testament

"I pray also that the eyes of your heart be enlightened in order that you may know the hope to which he has called you, the riches of his glorious inheritance in the saints, and his incomparably great power for us who believe." (Ephesians 1:18-19)

Power Within	Reference	Text
Mary	Luke 1:35	The angel answered, "The Holy Spirit will upon you, and the power of the Most High will overshadow you. So the holy one to be born will be called the Son of God."
Jesus	Luke 6:19	And the people all tried to touch him, because power was coming from him and healing them all.
Disciples	Luke 9:1	When Jesus had called the Twelve together, he gave them power and authority to drive out all demons and to cure diseases.
Gospel	Romans 1:16	I am not ashamed of the gospel, because it is the power of God for the salvation of everyone who believes.
Jesus at the 2nd coming	Mark 13:26	At that time men will see the Son of Man coming in clouds with great power and glory.
Believers	Romans 15:13	May the God of hope fill you with all joy and peace as you trust in him, so that you may overflow with hope by the power of the Holy Spirit.
Eternal Life	Philippians 3:21	who, by the power that enables him to bring everything under his control, will transform our lowly bodies so that they will be like his glorious body.

How different the New Testament message of power seems to me. I see the power of healing, hope, joy, peace and salvation. In that is the confidence of our faith. Truly this is the power that God has designed to be within each of us. He is the source of all power. We can look forward to joining the chorus of chosen ones. "After this I heard what sounded like the roar of a great multitude in heaven shouting: 'Hallelujah! Salvation and glory and power belong to our God.'" (Revelations 19:1)

Milestone #30

Rest your faith on God's power.

1. How would you describe God's power as reported in the Old Testament? Why do you think God's power was so often demonstrated in warring conflicts between the Israelites and their enemies?

2. Read Matthew 12:22-28. What miracle did Jesus perform? What was the response of the crowd? The Pharisees? What was the real source of Jesus' power to perform the miracle? Can power that is divided be in conflict? What would be the result if it were?

3. How would you describe God's power as reported in the New Testament? How does it differ from the Old Testament? Do any of the wars of the twentieth century reflect the workings of God's power? Explain.

4. What does the concept of faith mean to you? Have you seen faith work in your life? What makes faith difficult for you?

5. What specific area of your life are you in need of God's power? What principles or disciplines would help you exercise your faith if they were followed?

6. Read 2 Timothy 1:7. What does it mean not to be timid? How does this relate to a spirit of power? To the qualities of love and self-discipline? What is the source of power for believers? Do you have this power? Explain.

Light

"Granny-Mommy isn't the light beautiful?"

The question came from our grandson, Ryan. Yvonne and he were sitting on the lawn of the White House watching the fireworks on the evening of July 4, 1992. Ryan had traveled from California to spend ten days with us, and we were enjoying every minute of it. This night was special. We were visiting Bruce and Kathy for a couple of days, and Kathy's sister, Janice, had arranged for two admission tickets for viewing of the fireworks display from the Rose Garden of the White House.

Bruce, Kathy and I had dropped off Yvonne and Ryan at the White House and we then sought parking near the Reflecting Pool, close to the Washington Monument. We felt that would provide the best unobstructed view of the fireworks. Indeed the show was spectacular. The crowds of people were spellbound by the display of color, forms and bursts of energy. For me, there was no reminder of the bombardments of any war, but rather, the happy celebration of a blessed nation. It was as though God's light was falling upon us as we sat by the pool in awe of the splendor before us.

For Yvonne and Ryan, the uniqueness of being at the White House to witness this brought added pleasure to the occasion. The festivities included refreshments, souvenirs, entertainment from the clowns, and costumed people representing past presidents and first ladies. It is a wonderful memory that Yvonne holds dear in her heart. It was a time of sharing between Yvonne and Ryan.

There were other July 4th's that held fond memories. In 1991, the Persian Gulf War was still a recent memory. Michael, Cheryl and Ryan were visiting. Bruce and Kathy and Stephanie also joined us for the holiday. It was a day of picnicking with the family. It was a special day of happiness for we hadn't seen

Michael since before Operation Desert Storm. He was home, safe. We could see him, talk with him, and hug him. We went to a fireworks display in the area. How much these reminded me of the sights I had seen on television of the real fireworks that occurred in Irag a few months before. But later, the fireworks that Bruce had brought and set off in our backyard caused tears of happiness to flow. The family was together. There was laughter and love and a moment of peace.

Still earlicr, I recall the fireworks at Williamsburg when Yvonne and I visited Michael and his family in Newport News. Our visits to Williamsburg were always a pleasure. But on July 4th, the parades, activities and fireworks brought on a strong sense of patriotism. It brings a sense of pride to be in this country at this time.

Then I go back fifty years and recall the occasions that Dad would take me out on a small boat on the Patapsco River and watch the fireworks bursting above our heads from Fort McHenry. In the quiet and dark stillness of the waters, there were sudden and momentary bursts of light. I vividly remember Dad talking of the battle that took place there in 1812 and how important it was to our young country. I remember how the light cast differing shadows across the face of Dad. It was as though he suddenly appeared from nowhere and then just as suddenly disappeared. Each appearance was different than the one before, and yet each was the same. It was comforting to see him in the changing light, but his voice told me he was there in the darkness also.

Types of Light

"And we have the word of the prophets made ore certain, and you will do well to pay attention to it, as to a light shining in a dark place, until the day dawns and the morning star rises in your hearts." (2 Peter 1:19)

Type of Light	Reference	Text
Physical	Genesis 1:3-4	And God said, "Let there be light," and there was light. God saw that the light was good, and he separated light from the darkness.
God's	Isaiah 60:20	Your sun will never set again, and your moon will wane no more; the Lord will be your everlasting light, and your days of sorrow will end.
Christ's	John 8:12	When Jesus spoke again to the people, he said, "I am the light of the world. Whoever follows me will never walk in darkness, but will have the light of life."
Holy Spirit	Isaiah 60:1-2	"Arise, shine, for your light has come, and the glory of the Lord rises upon you. See, darkness covers the earth and thick darkness is over the peoples, but the Lord rises upon you and his glory appears over you."
The Word	Psalm 119:130	The unfolding of your words gives light; it gives understanding to the simple.
Early	Revelations 22:16	"I, Jesus, have sent my angel to give you this testimony for the churches. I am the Root and the Offspring of David, and the bright Morning Star."
Late	John 12:35-36	Then Jesus told them, "You are going to have the light just a little while longer. Walk while you have the light, before darkness overtakes you. The man who walks in the dark does not know where he is going. Put your trust in the light while you have it, so that you may become sons of light."
Reflective	1 John 2:8-10	Yet I am writing you a new command; its truth is seen in him and you, because the darkness is passing and the true light is already shining. Anyone who claims to be in the light but hates his brother is still in the darkness. Whoever loves his brother lives in the light, and there is nothing in him to make him stumble.

The properties of light are three-fold and, therefore, remind me of the Trinity. We generally define light as rays. First, there is the red, or heat, ray. It is felt, but not seen. Much as God the Father. Then, there is the yellow, or light, ray. It is seen, but not felt. Much as the living Word, the Son, declares the Father. Finally, there is the blue, or chemical, ray. It is neither felt or seen. Its presence is made known by the effect of a chemical action which produces change, such as in photography. Much as the Holy Spirit is made known by its wondrous works and the changes it brings in people.

Artists and photographers often seek out the early light and/or the late light. Objects seem to take on a different dimension in those lights. I see Jesus as the Morning Star bringing new vision to those that see His light. I see, also, Jesus as the late light for we have been told that our time will end without warning and we are to walk in His light while it is still available to us. Each person is but an object to reflect the Light from above. To reflect that light though, we must walk in the light.

Milestone #31

Walk in the Light.

1. What does the term "light at the end of the tunnel" mean to you? Give an example of how this applied to you. Were you chasing the light or was it approaching you? What difference
, if any, does this make?

2. In your own words, define the various forms of light identified in the chart, Types of Light. Which one do you feel is most meaningful to you? Why?

3. John 3:21 states that "whoever lives by the truth comes into the light." What does it mean to live by the truth? Who judges what is true? How do you know if you live by the truth?

4. Read again 1 John 2:8-10. How do you now define walking in the light? Does this differ any from your answer to question 3. above? How?

5. What was Jesus' new command? What does it mean to love your brother (neighbor, etc.)? Do you believe you can truly say you love your neighbor? What, if anything, is preventing you from loving your neighbor? How can you better demonstrate this love?

6. Read Psalm 19:8, 119:105; Proverbs 6:23. How does one learn to walk in the light? Are there other sources for knowing you are walking in the light? Explain.

Water

A late summer hurricane was active in the Atlantic. Rain, wind and pounding surf were beating along the Ocean City coastline. It figures. I rarely take any extended vacation time, and now that we have the family here and the ocean front motel room paid for, we have to sit and watch a storm. Fortunately, our good friends, Jim and Olga, are also here in the adjoining room. There will be no beach time for a couple of days, but we will have the companionship of our friends. Hopefully, our children will not get too restless.

It appeared as if the storm would surely ruin the vacation for all of us. That evening, we went to dinner and passed the building site of a new condominium on the boardwalk. We talked about the ideal location of the building, and wondered about the appearance of the individual units. As the storm raged on the next day, we went to the condominium to take the tour. The more we saw, the more we liked it. Elevators were not operating yet in this six story structure. When the sales representative told us they had an end unit on the top, I just had to see that unit. The whole family climbed the stairs; the first climb of several over the next couple of days. What a wonderful view from the top floor of that unfinished unit. A panorama of quieting sea before us gave me a sense of belonging. From the back, we could view the entire back bay, and from the side a view of the sprawling north beach development.

The last thing that we did before leaving our vacation site was to put a deposit on the top floor, end unit. Now, looking back, I can see how the fury of the storm brought us years of enjoyment in our "second home". For me, the fury turned to calmness. That ocean view became my tranquilizer. If only all the storms in one's life could result in such endings. The force of water can, and does, cause change. I could have viewed that incident as a lost vacation, but in doing so, I would have lost all the joy from the following years. It was but the first step in achieving some happiness.

Floods, tidal waves, hurricanes bring disaster from the force of
the water. Not many people would have the opportunity to bring
a happy ending to those tragedies. The flood story from the
Bible speaks to that. Only Noah and his family were saved,
along with a pairing of the animals. But from that a new beginning for mankind. At the age of two, our grandson, Ryan,
noticed a rainbow in the sky. He pointed and said, "Look!" We
told him about the rainbow and how it was a reminder to us of
God's promise not to flood the earth again. The rainbow was a
happy ending to a storm. As he watched, the rainbow seemed to
fade away, and he said, "Do it again." We discussed the story of
the flood with Ryan again. This time he got excited about the
animals coming two-by-two. For awhile his favorite saying was
"two-by-two".

The water doesn't always come with destructive force. As a
penetrating rain it brings growth to all things of the earth. As a
gentle rain, it is refreshing to the senses. In fact, our granddaughter, Sarah Anne, likes to stand in the rain and have it touch
her face.

Our son, Michael, brought some perspective to water when he
recently wrote to me. His thoughts were:

"All life revolves around water. In my years of hunting, I've
learned that I must first find the source of water in the area. I
have sought water for all types of game: quail, rabbits, frogs,
squirrels, ducks, deer, bear, raccoon, muskrat. In every case I
have been successful when I hunted water. Slow, floating
trips along the rivers made boundless game visible. Early
morning hours were particularly noteworthy. The sun and the
light of day are never more beautiful than as it rises or sets on
a duck blind — or on the ocean as my surf rod points to the
orange orb in long arching casts.

"People are drawn to water. Millions flock to the coastal
beaches or land locked bays and lakes to spend their vaca-

tions. It was those early vacations that love of the ocean developed within as I worked at overcoming the tendency toward seasickness and sought a vocation on the water."

Water is needed for survival. We can only be without it for a couple of days. It is the sustenance of life. God understands our thirst and provides for us. The following table demonstrates God's care:

Sustenance of Life

"On that day living water will flow out from Jerusalem, half to the eastern sea and half to the western sea, in summer and in winter. The Lord will be king over the whole earth. On that day there will be one Lord, and his name the only name." (Zechariah 14:8-9)

Provision	Reference	Text
At creation	Genesis 1:1-2	In the beginning God created the heavens and earth. Now the earth was formless and empty, darkness was over the surface of the deep, and the Spirit of God was hovering over the waters.
In need	Numbers 20:7-8	The Lord said to Moses, "Take the staff, and you and your brother Aaron gather the assembly together. Speak to the rock before their eyes and it will pour out its water. You will bring water out of the rock for the community so they and their livestock can drink."
Refusal to accept	Jeremiah 2:13	My people have committed two sins: They have forsaken me, the spring of living water, and have dug their own cisterns, broken cisterns that cannot hold water.
Sharing	Mark 9:41	I tell you the truth, anyone who gives you a cup of water in my name because you belong to Christ will certainly not lose his reward.
Satisfaction	John 7:37-38	On the last and greatest day of the Feast, Jesus stood and said in a loud voice, "If anyone is thirsty, let him come to me and drink. Whoever believes in me, as the scripture has said, streams of living water will flow from within him.
Eternal	John 4:13-14	Jesus answered, "Everyone who drinks this water will be thirsty again, but whoever drinks the water I give him will never thirst. Indeed, the water I give him will become in him a spring of water welling up to eternal life."

I look to Jesus' first miracle and it was the changing of water into wine (John 2:8-10). It displayed his mastery over nature. Later he stilled the turbulent sea (Matthew 8:26), and still later, he walked on the surface of the water (Matthew 14:25). This compares with the power of God in creation and the control of the elements in the parting of the Red Sea (Exodus 14:16) and the parting of the Jordan River (Joshua 3:17).

Michael's recent letter to me ended with the following: "On earth, water is life. In heaven, Christ is our eternal drink of water, our eternal life. The need for water is essential to those things which live. How ironic that man chooses not to drink from the cup which overflows. Ponce-de-Leon sought the eternal fountain of youth. Too bad he didn't recognize the God which he proclaimed provided for the eternal fountain of life."

From Psalm 23: "...he leads me beside the still waters, he restores my soul...my cup overflows."

Milestone #32

Drink from the spring of living water.

1. What are the uses of water that you can identify? Which use is the most important to you? Why? Are any of the uses harmful? Explain.

2. How does man harness water to use for his purpose? Do any of these methods cause damage to the environment? Explain. If so, what would you do to change the method of harnessing, or use of, water?

3. The Bible states that God, through Moses, parted the Red Sea and later, through Joshua, parted the Jordan River. What do these acts mean to you? If they did not occur, would it have any impact on your faith? If they were scientifically demonstrated, would it have any impact on your faith? Explain.

4. How did Jesus demonstrate His control over water? How do you think He accomplished this? By what power did He accomplish these acts? Do you believe He did these acts?

5. Read again John 4:13-14. Describe in your own words what Jesus is saying. Is He referring to water as defined in question 1. above? Explain.

6. Read Isaiah 55:1, Revelations 22:17. Who is invited to satisfy their thirst? Have you been invited? Why, or why not? Have you taken of the free gift of life?

Bread

Meals have always been a focal point of our family life. It was an opportunity for everyone to share the events of the day and the dreams of tomorrow. Whether it was the formal setting of a special occasion, a more casual setting of the typical day, an outside picnic setting, or the chaotic hustle of grabbing a snack before running off in different directions, the family fellowship of the meal brought a bonding to the family. Often this family was the extended family that included our friends and acquaintances.

Our children have often commented about the often spontaneous meals we have had with our neighbors. Crab feasts and clam bakes were particularly memorable as these were generally all day events. Our families would gather in the backyard and each family contributed one or more courses to the meal. One or two gas grills would be going all day with either hot dogs or hamburgers or sausage or steaks. Depending on availability, a steamer would be cooking on an open pit with Chesapeake Bay blue crabs or littleneck clams or lobsters. Yvonne's homemade crab soup was a must. Potato salad, cole slaw, corn on the cob and special dishes would fill the menu.

Horseshoes, badminton, basketball and bocchi ball were the games of choice. In fact, we setup outside lights for the horseshoe pits so we could continue the games into the night. Those events were filled with conversation, story-telling and much laughter. It was a time of sharing, a time of fellowship, a time of bonding. The bonding has obviously held for, as the children moved on and the neighbors moved away, we have maintained a continuing relationship with all of those dear friends.

I remember the years that my father would join us for a Saturday morning breakfast. Yvonne would busy herself at the griddle making pancakes as fast as she could with the bacon and sausage frying alongside. Bruce and Michael were boys growing into young men and could consume a considerable amount of food.

The pancake stacks were very impressive and even more impressive was the fact that they cleaned their plates.

We talked about the events of the week, but mostly we listened to Dad tell stories of times past. He kept us very entertained. Over time we noticed a bit of embellishment in the stories, and that made them all the more enjoyable the next time we heard them. Our sons have often said we should have recorded those conversations. For now they are family stories that can not be told again, entertainment that can not be repeated, a fellowship that is now fond memories.

Our home was always the center of special occasions. Each Christmas Eve the entire family and many close friends would join us for buffet dinner. It was not unusual to have 40 to 50 people there. I don't know how Yvonne was able to handle the preparation of all that food. As the women were busy setting out the meal, the men were in the basement at the pool table participating in team challenge pool or just watching the action. The festivities paused long enough for everyone to attend midnight mass, and then some portion of the crowd would return for a snack and some more billiards. The happiness and closeness felt at those times was almost overwhelming. So many fond memories of everyone linger on in my mind.

Several events a year like this would occur in our home and we enjoyed everyone of them. Of course, we were exhausted at the effort, but that is not part of our memories. Only the joy and happiness of the fellowship remains.

When Michael was attending the Naval Academy, we were living just about ten miles from Annapolis. It was not uncommon for us to have a house full of midshipmen on Saturday afternoons. There was always a large pot of sausage and peppers, or beef barbecue on the stove. Food at the Academy was wonderful, yet these young men and women preferred to get away for a few hours for fellowship that had no rules and boundaries. The confusion of those days added much to our joy of those years.

The Naval Academy provided me many great memories, and some of those are centered around meals. Occasionally, Michael would invite me to a mid-week breakfast at the Academy. And what a breakfast it would be: steak, eggs, hash brown potatoes, bacon, sausage and more. They even had dessert for breakfast: Ice cream, pies, fruit and the list goes on. Each trip there I became more impressed at the ability to serve 4,000 people at one setting and have all the food served hot. Knowing that these young men and women were on their good behavior, I was still impressed by their social conduct and good manners.

Another memorable meal at the Academy was Thanksgiving dinner in 1980. My father and Yvonne's mother joined Yvonne, Bruce, Stephanie and me as we visited Michael. We all had dinner together in Bancroft Hall. The meal was indescribably good. In addition to the carved turkey, everything imaginable was served. While this may be termed a banquet for the masses, it had the elements of a close family gathering. The midshipmen openly shared their experiences, and it seemed as though we had known them for years. Dad was very impressed and emotionally overjoyed at the experience. He spoke of it often.

There are many other special meals away from home that hold a place in my heart. The joyous wedding feasts of our children are certainly at the top of the list. Each of these is in itself a happy story. Also, there are the quiet meals that Yvonne and I share at a favorite restaurant, or the visit to a neighbor and friend. The breaking of bread with someone makes the meal special. I sometimes forget that every meal is an opportunity to bond closer to ones you are sharing with at the time. It is so easy to take for granted the individuals that are by your side each day. Even in writing this chapter, I feel a need to increase my aware-ness of the opportunity that the everyday meal provides. I must commit to making it a time of fellowship with my dear wife.

There are many biblical stories about the fellowship of meals. Abraham greeted the strangers by offering them a meal. Jesse sent David to Saul with the gift of food for a meal. Jesus relaxed in the company of his friends with a meal. Of course, Jesus said good-bye to his friends with the Last Supper. There is plenty of precedence in using the meal to nourish the body as well as nurturing friendship.

Miraculous feedings are also noted in the Bible. God sent manna and quail to the wandering Jewish nation (Exodus 16:12-18), Elisha fed 100 (2 Kings 4:42-44), Jesus fed 5,000 (Matthew 14:16-21) and then 4,000 (Matthew 15:33-38). These were certainly special events.

No matter the circumstances, there are certain principles of nourishment that should be constantly before us. The following table outlines these thoughts:

Principles of Nourishment

"Then the angel said to me, 'Write: Blessed are those who are invited to the wedding supper of the Lamb!' And he added, 'These are the true words of God.'" (Revelation 19:9)

Principle	Reference	Text
Source	Genesis 1:29	"Then God said, 'I give you every seed-bearing plant on the face of the whole earth and every tree that has fruit with seed in it. They will be yours for food.'"
	Genesis 9:3	"Everything that lives and moves will be food for you. Just as I gave you the green plants, I now give you everything."
Provision	Psalm 145:15	"The eyes of all look to you, and you give them their food at the proper time."
	Matthew 6:26	"Look at the birds of the air; they do not sow or reap or store away in barns, and yet your heavenly Father feeds them. Are you not much more valuable they they?"
Request	Matthew 6:11	"Give us today our daily bread."
	Matthew 7:9	"Which of you, if his son asks for bread, will give him a stone?"
Act of fellowship	Acts 2:42	"They devoted themselves to the apostles' teaching and to the fellowship, to the breaking of the bread and to prayer."
	Acts 27:35-36	"Then he broke it and began to eat. They were all encouraged and ate some food themselves."
The word as food	Deuteronomy 8:3	"He humbled you, causing you to hunger and then feeding you with manna, which neither you nor your fathers had known, to teach you that man does not live on bread alone but on every word that comes from the mouth of the Lord."
	Jeremiah 15:16	"When your words came, I ate them; they were my joy and my heart's delight, for I bear your name, O Lord God Almighty."
Spiritual food	John 6:51	"I am the living bread that came down from heaven. If anyone eats of this bread, he will live forever. This bread is my flesh, which I will give for the life of the world."
	Mark 14:22	"While they were eating, Jesus took bread, gave thanks and broke it, and gave it to his disciples, saying, 'Take it; this is my body.'"

Jesus placed great emphasis on meals. Not only by the example of sitting in fellowship with His followers, but in the parables that He taught, such as, the leavened bread (Matthew 13:33), the wedding feast (Matthew 22:2-14), the barren fig tree (Luke 13:6-9) and the great supper (Luke 14:16-24). His presence, His words, His example, His sacrifice all bring meaning to the nourishment of my body and soul.

The Holy Eucharist is important in my life as it nourishes my spiritual being along with the Word. My daily meals nourish my physical body to provide me the strength to serve my God.

Milestone #33

Regard each meal as an act of fellowship.

1. Do you enjoy eating alone? Do you eat alone often? Would you rather eat alone or with others? Why?

2. Describe a meal that you particularly remember? Were you the host or an invited guest? What made that meal special? What elements of that event would you like to replicate often? Why?

3. How would you describe your typical family meal? Is it an environment you would want your friends to be involved in? Why? What subjects are generally discussed at your family meals? Are any subjects avoided? Do the children partici- pate in the discussion? How do you feel about the discussions at your typical family meals?

4. Read Luke 22:14-38. What did Jesus and His disciples discuss at the Last Supper? How does this compare with discussions you have at special meals with family and/or friends? Do you discuss your future, your politics, your ambition, your needs, your faith?

5. Your physical body is certainly nourished by the meals you have. Is this an appropriate time to nourish your relationship with others? Is it appropriate to sit and talk after eating rather than quickly leave the table to wash dishes and clean-up? Do you get involved in the conversation or just take a passive interest?

6. Do you feel that fellowship during a meal is necessary? Desired? How can you make each meal an act of fellowship?

Performance

Sin

For a number of years our family spent vacation time together at a Christian camp located in Western Maryland. Each and every year was a wonderful experience. It was a time of relaxation, recreation, fellowship and meditation. Distractions from the secular life were put aside for a joyful week. No newspapers or television or telephone to consume the precious moments of each day.

There were activities for the family and separate activities for adults, teenagers, children and infants. There were daily devotions and Bible study and time for private contemplation. The setting was beautiful, set in the wooded hills of Frederick County. In particular, the chapel sat on a rocky summit that overlooked the Potomac River seen in the distant rolling countryside. How easy it was to feel close to God, close to nature, close to oneself.

This was a time for sharing with others and getting closer to people in a week than with our neighbors and other friends that we had known for years. From the fellowship in that vacation experience more than twenty years ago, we built life-long friendships. On reflection, our son, Michael, said that he remembers having the hope that he would grow up to have the kind of friends that we had at family camp.

There are a number of instances that come to mind when I reflect on those times. The dozen or so families that would attend the vacation camp participated by taking responsibility for preparing and directing various activities. There was always something going on. I recall one night that was an especially clear night. A group of adults decided that they would do some star gazing through a telescope that someone had brought. After the children were put to bed, a small group gathered to take turns on the

telescope and see into the heavens. The friend that had brought
the telescope was a high school science teacher and had a strong
interest in astronomy. He guided our view of the heavens. As
the stars moved across the sky, it was necessary to move the
telescope to get a better view of a particular formation or heavenly body. Time passed and the group got a bit smaller. The
silent wonder of the sky and the quiet discussion the small group
was having suddenly was interrupted by bright lights and the
rumble of a noisy engine. It was the pre-dawn encroachment of
the milk delivery truck. As startled as that small group may have
been, I wondered at the surprise the truck driver must have felt to
see several people laying on their backs in the middle of the
roadway with heads together and extended bodies making an
ever increasing circle. The topic of conversation that day was
the all night star watching activity and its abrupt ending.
That memory has been refreshed in my mind due to the recent
interest my sons have in astronomy. On a recent Christmas,
Bruce's wife, Kathy, gave him a telescope and he, in his usual
manner, immersed himself into study: the study of the stars.
This was something he shared with his brother, Michael. Even
though they are separated by the width of this country, they
communicate regularly on their findings in the heavens. On
most clear nights, they are out watching the stars; Michael laying
on the slanted roof of his house in California with binoculars and
Bruce on the deck at his home in Virginia gazing through his
telescope. It is a sharing that they have together. In a way, it
brings them close to each other in spite of the 3,000 miles that
separate them.

On one of those summer jaunts to family camp, I volunteered to
lead the teenagers in their activities and Bible studies. As the
weeks drew near to vacation time, I gathered the materials and
designed the template to make mosaic hot plates with a Christian
theme pattern, developed a skit for the teenagers to present to the
total group on the last evening of the camp, prepared for discussion of specific moral issues that I felt teenagers faced, and the
like. Once I got together with the teenagers, some of the planned

discussions were put aside as we explored items of particular interest to them. I was surprised to find that they were concerned about sin and its impact on their life after life. It never occurred to me that teenagers thought anything about eternal life and certainly not about the impact of sin on that life.

One morning I announced to the group that we were going to have an afternoon campfire gathering and they were to bring their marshmallows. When we gathered at the selected site, I had some of the group gather wood and we started our small campfire. After devotions, I had everyone gather two small sticks and a small vine. The teenagers were then told to make a cross from the twigs and vine. I then passed out notepaper and pencils and asked each teenager to write down a wrongdoing, or sin, that they could recall. When they had completed that, they were told to attach their sin to the cross. We then circled the campfire and sang some familiar hymns. Each teenager was told to place their cross in the campfire. As the fire blazed, I explained that this was walking in the Light. Their sins were nailed to the cross with Jesus, and His resurrection consumed their sin on a very personal basis. We then sang hymns of praise.

The teenagers responded very favorably to this; however, some of the parents were concerned when they heard about it. The parents asked me if this wasn't some sort of sacrificial ceremony. I responded with questions to them. "Don't you believe that Jesus' sacrifice was necessary to end all sacrificial ceremonies? Don't you believe that Jesus' death on the cross provided for the forgiveness of all our sins, past, present and future? Don't you see that this was a visual representation of Jesus' work in our lives?" Following the discussion, I became concerned about the attitude those parents had toward their own sin, and I prayed that they may have the insight their children demonstrated.

What is sin? The word is a medieval archery term. An archer would shoot at a target and a spotter would shout out "sin" if the arrow missed the mark. So it can be said, to sin is to miss the mark. Isaiah (53:6) puts it this way, "We all, like sheep, have gone astray, each of us has turned his own way; and the Lord has laid on him the iniquity of us all." Paul in his letter to the Romans (14:23) states, "...everything that does not come from faith is sin."

Sin, then, is the result of actions and attitudes done to please self and not God. Sin is the attitude of not trusting God in any particular area of your life. The word faith means to trust in, or rely upon. When we trust in and rely upon God for everything in our lives, we will have the confidence that "...all that happens is working for our good if we love God and are fitting into His plans." (Romans 8:28). Thus if there is an area of our lives in which we are not trusting and relying upon God, that is sin. Disobeying God's law is sin! "Anyone, then, who knows the good he ought to do and doesn't do it, sins." (James 4:17)

What causes people to sin? This is called temptation. In the Garden of Eden, Eve was tempted. In the wilderness, Jesus was tempted. Each day we are all tempted in the elements of worldliness.

TEMPTATION

"No temptation has seized you except what is common to man. And God is faithful; he will not let you be tempted beyond what you can bear. But when you are tempted, he will also provide a way out so that you can stand up under it." (1 Corinthians 10:13)

Element	Eve Genesis 3:6	Jesus Luke 4:3-12	Worldliness 1 John 2:17
Bodily	"good for food"	"tell this stone to become bread"	"cravings of sinful man"
Emotional	"pleasing to the eye"	"give you all authority and splendor"	"lust of his eyes"
Intellectual	"desirable for giving wisdom"	"If you are the Son of God, throw yourself down from here"	"boasting of what he does"

It is not so much that one is tempted; it is one's response to temptation. Eve gave in to temptation, and sinned. Jesus resisted temptation, and was righteous. Each of us respond differently to each situation. We need to follow the example that Jesus gave and listen to the advice of John (1 John 3:7): "Dear children, do not let anyone lead you astray. He who does what is right is righteous, just as he is righteous."

Righteous life and a life of sin are, in idea, mutually exclusive. Sin in the Christian is either involuntary (weakness) or in acknowledged contradiction to the ruling principle of their life (habitual). "For all have sinned and fall short of the glory of God." (Romans 3:23). Following is a partial list of sins:

TYPES OF SIN
Galations 5:16-21

Sins of Attitude	Sins of Action
sexual immorality (eagerness for lustful pleasures)	debauchery (to corrupt or seduce others)
impurity (impure thoughts)	idolatry
hatred	witchcraft (spiritualism)
jealousy	discord (fighting)
fits of rage (anger)	selfish ambition (constant effort to get the best for yourself)
factions (feeling that everyone else is wrong except those in your own group)	dissension (complaints and criticism)
envy	drunkenness and orgies (wild parties)

Sin is not just a matter of acts such as cheating, lying, being immoral, etc. These actions are the results of a sinful attitude. The sin within yourself will lead to wrongdoing against others. It is powerfully obvious that sin is devastating in its impact, and Scripture warns us about its destructive results. "I warn you, as I did before, that those who live like this will not inherit the kingdom of God." (Galations 5:21). The words, "those who live like this", indicate performing repeatedly or habitually as distinguished from a single action. This is not to take away from the wrong of the single action, but rather to give us hope if we are willing to change and avoid continuing the sin.

Milestone #34

Resist temptation and trust in God's protection.

1. How would you describe sin? Are there different levels of sin? On a scale of 0 to 10 (0 = no sin, 10 = most severe sin), rank your feeling as to the seriousness of sin, and explain your ranking:

> ___ Murder another person
> ___ Getting angry with someone
> ___ Telling an "outright" lie
> ___ Telling a "white" lie
> ___ Falsely accusing someone
> ___ Looking up answers on completing a crossword puzzle
> ___ Wanting something someone else has

2. How would you describe a sin of attitude? Is this different than a sin of action? Explain.

3. Why do you feel Jesus allowed himself to be tempted? What was Satan's purpose in tempting Jesus?

4. Do you sense the devil tempting you? In what way? Does knowing that Jesus was tempted help you in your Christian life? How? Can Jesus identify with your temptation (Hebrews 4:15)?

5. Read Matthew 7:11, Psalm 107:8-9. How has God provided for you most recently? Were you tempted to deny his provision? In what way?

6. Has God protected you recently? How? Are you trusting Him for protection today? How? Read Psalm 91. Analyze and discuss each verse relative to God's protection of you today.

Guilt

Our daughter, Stephanie, has told us that she believes a lot of people are living a life that is controlled by guilt. She said that it probably is hard for us to understand what that means, but she can relate to it because that is the way she lived her life for many years.

From the time that Stephanie was in her early teens, she reacted negatively against any discipline that her mother or I would try to impose on her. She grew more rebellious as the years passed by; she seemed to be doing things just to declare her independence. We did not realize that these small acts of rebellion were building a guilt complex within her. When she encountered trials and tribulations, she interpreted this as a sign from God that her disobedience has resulted in punishment to her. Stephanie by now has transferred the guilt complex from feeling badly about disappointing her parents to feeling badly about disappointing God.

Difficulties in her life were becoming greater. She then made the self-determination that no matter what she did, she could not improve her situation. This led to a lowering of her standards to seek a level were she felt she could be accepted more easily. But each time she lowered her standards, she seemed to have more and more problems. Stephanie believed she was in a downward spiral and she had no hope of ever changing her quality of life. She was in a trap that she could not escape from. Being the caring person that she is, she was seeking someone to help but her guilt feelings were causing her to lower her standards so she could find someone to accept her. Her lower standards led her to do things that increased the guilty feelings. And the cycle continued.

Stephanie tried to reach out for help. Her calls home increased. When we sensed trouble, we would respond with a visit to take her out of her environment for a short period, or we would send some financial aid. We didn't understand her problem and were slow to see the emerging pattern. We were at a loss for what to do and, both Yvonne and I, prayed that Jesus take control of her

life. Yvonne talked to Stephanie about reading the Bible and told
her of certain passages that had meaning to Yvonne. Stephanie
expressed interest in the Bible and we gave her one on our next
visit. She began to read the Bible. As she has explained it, she
was looking for answers to specific problems. She needed a
quick fix and searched for the words that would direct her. No
answers came to her.

Shortly after her daughter was born, she was going through the
motions of reading the Bible. There wasn't any kind of plan to
her reading pattern. It was more a random opening of the book
and reading a few passages. However, she felt the need to pray
for her daughter. She doesn't remember what she prayed, but
she knows it brought her the realization that she had to stop
depending on others to accept her. She had to accept herself
first. But how could she do that? There were so many wrong
things she had done; so many people she had hurt; a vengeful
God that was punishing her.

Quietly, without great excitement or breath-taking vision, she
realized that Jesus had sacrificed Himself so that her sins could
be forgiven. As Stephanie described it, "I finally saw the suffering of Jesus, I felt the pain of the nails driven into His body, I
shared the anguish of His Mother witnessing His death. That
scene became very real to me. And all of that was because He
loved me enough to die for me."

Now she knew her past sins, her present sins, and even her future
sins would be forgiven if she would only accept Him as her
Savior. Then by accepting Him, she found she could accept
herself. She acknowledged the wrong she had done. The guilt
was indeed there, but the feeling of guilt, the guilt complex,
slowly drifted away. With the barriers of guilt now gone,
Stephanie began to climb from the depths she had lowered
herself. She learned, and is still learning, what freedom from
guilt is all about. Her quality of life is improving. She is
reaching out to others: not for acceptance from them, but rather

to serve them. It is not an easy process. She had to reach out to her God, and in turn, God reached out to help her and answer her anguish.

FREEDOM FROM GUILT

"Even if I were innocent, my mouth would condemn me; if I were blameless, it would pronounce me guilty." (Job 9:20)

Condition of Sin		Solution to Guilt	
Text	**Reference**	**Text**	**Reference**
The Lord saw how great man's wickedness had become, and that every inclination of the thoughts of his heart was filled with pain.	Genesis 6:5	He has not dealt with us according to our sins, nor rewarded us according to our iniquities. For high as the heavens are above the earth, so great is His loving kindness toward those who fear Him. As far as the east is from the west, so far has He removed our transgressions from us.	Psalm 103: 10-12
My guilt has overwhelmed me like a burden too heavy to bear.	Psalm 38:4	It was for freedom that Christ set us free; therefore keep standing firm and do not be subject again to a yoke of slavery.	Galations 5:1
But whoever fails to find me harms himself; all who hate me find death.	Proverbs 8:36	Therefore, there is now no condemnation for those who are in Christ Jesus, because through Christ Jesus the law of the Spirit of life set me free from the law of sin and death.	Romans 8:1
This is the verdict: Light has come into the world, but men loved darkness instead of light because their sins were evil.	John 3:19	But whoever lives by the truth comes into the light, so that it may be seen plainly that what he has done has been done through God.	John 3:21
....worldly sorrow brings death.	1 Corinthians 7:10	Godly sorrow brings repentance that leads to salvation and leaves no regret....	1 Corinthians 7:10

The good news is that everyone can be freed from the bindings of guilt that accompany wrongdoing.

What is guilt? The dictionary defines it as, "The state of one who, by violation of law, has made himself deserving of punishment." In other words, by not being obedient, you bear the risk of punishment; and guilt is carrying the threat of punishment. "Everyone who sins breaks the law; in fact, sin is lawlessness." (1 John 3:4). Guilt is the result of sin.

As Job knows that his own words condemn him, so do we experience that self-condemnation. Do our actions reflect what we say? The struggle within us is the temptation to sin. So often do we succumb to that temptation. But God provides for us relief from guilt and the fear of judgment. If you are a Christian, your sins are forgiven. You don't have to carry the guilt of sin. The perfect sacrifice has been made that brings total forgiveness of our sins and acceptance by God. We can experience that total acceptance and love. We can be released from our poor performance and made free to love and forgive others. We can have freedom from guilt and be made free to love self and life.

Milestone #35

Stand firm in your faith and be kept free from guilt.

1. How do you define guilt? What is the difference, if any, between being guilty and feeling guilty?

2. What is the purpose of our laws of society? Have you disobeyed any of these laws? Explain. What risk did you, or would you, have in disobeying these laws? How did you feel in disobeying any of these laws?

3. What was the purpose of God's laws? Have you disobeyed any of God's laws? How do you know if you are disobeying God? How did you feel about yourself in disobeying any of God's laws?

4. What do you believe "freedom from guilt" means? Do you consider yourself free from guilt? Why, or why not? Is there anything you must do to be free from guilt? If so, what?

5. Have you known anyone that was living a life filled with guilt? How was this feeling of guilt demonstrated to you? What was the attitude of the person? Their self-esteem? Their manner of speaking?

6. Do you feel you could help someone whose life is filled with guilt? If so, how?

Repentance

People can change, and they do change. As I look back over the lives of our children I see so much change in each of them. It is much easier to see change in others than in oneself. I'm sure I have changed, and this book reflects just some of the change that I have recognized. But as a typical parent and grandparent, it is my children, and my children's children, that I most enjoy thinking about and most easily talk about. So again, I reflect on them and certain changes I have noticed over the years.

All of our children grew up with the practice of going to church every Sunday. Yvonne and I worked diligently at instructing them in the precepts of the Christian faith. We like to believe they all had the same exposure, although I assume that is not entirely accurate, as Yvonne and I were surely changing during all those years. As children, Bruce, Michael and Stephanie all seemed to be developing the proper foundations of a righteous life. But indeed changes took place that we didn't anticipate.

Bruce, being the oldest, set out to make his own way at a early age. He seemed intent on testing the limits of all he knew and perceived. While at college, he began questioning the teachings of the church, and to a large degree, the teachings of his parents. He was seeking answers to all the great mysteries of the world, not the least of which was the presence of God. He spent time on studying the occult, and searching other religions for answers to his questions. The few times we talked of religion and philosophy during those years, Bruce would repeatedly say, "I believe in the First Cause; I believe that there is a Supreme Being. I am just not sure that the Bible is a true representation of God, or even if there is a life after this earthly existence."

Concerning Bruce's spiritual growth, he seemed to have many years of aimless wanderings. But yet we knew he was searching for the meaning of life and proof of the existence of God. Yvonne spent ten years praying fervently for him to find the path to God. When my father was in the hospital nearing death, Bruce found an article in a magazine about Billy Graham. He showed this to his mother and said, "Here is an article that you will be interested in. It speaks of the importance of believing in Jesus Christ so that you may have eternal life. In times like this, I so want to truly believe in an afterlife."

A gradual change was noticed in Bruce after that. Bruce said he would like to have a Bible. His brother quickly responded by giving him a study Bible and we added to that a reference companion book. We know that Bruce has periodically read from the Bible and studied the meaning of certain passages. Clear evidence of this is the blessing that he gave this past Easter before our evening meal, and a few weeks later the deeply moving eulogy he presented at his Uncle Frank's funeral services. The following excerpt from that eulogy reflects the awareness that Bruce now has of relativity of the Bible in guiding our lives:

"'I will instruct you and teach you in the way you should go; I will counsel you and watch over you.' (Psalm 32:8)

"As we look back on our lives, it's often difficult to attribute a lesson or learning to any single person — the good ones that we keep and which define us have many teachers and are continually reinforced and impressed upon us. I do know that Uncle Frank influenced me in many ways...

"I was lucky in that, among others, I had him as a role model. And as I grew, I came to see, and appreciate, more of him. From his quiet strength and steadiness came a sense of purpose and dependability. His gruff exterior hid a gentle man, whose respect and caring for all life — whether it be his plants, a puppy, or family member — made him one of the kindest men I know. He was a man of honer and principles, with the courage to hold himself to them. The discipline he admired in the military he brought to his life; a dedicated and tireless worker, he strove to make the most of himself and the life he provided for his family. I don't know exactly what Uncle Frank's relationship with the Lord was, but I do know it was extremely close. This seems only natural, for as an artist and craftsman, Uncle Frank was also a creator.

"'By the grace God has given me, I laid a foundation as an expert builder, and someone else is building on it. But each one should be careful how he builds. For no one can lay any foundation other than the one already laid, which is Jesus Christ.' (1 Corinthians 3:10-11)

"With an artist's eye and appreciation, he always noticed things that others didn't. His gifted hands brought the beauty he saw to life so that we, too, could share in his discovery. A hawk in flight; a bird's wing; a rustic barn; a lone wolf; a colonial street; a cherished pet. He never fully appreciated the effect his works had on us and our perceptions of the world. He only saw his mistakes. We saw only his talent.

"This is much the same way that God views us as his creations. We see only our imperfections. God sees our promise... While we will miss Uncle Frank, and grieve his loss, we can be thankful that we were blessed with the opportunity for him to enrich our lives. We can be secure in our faith that we will meet him again. And we can rejoice that Uncle Frank has gone onto a greater place, having lived a complete life, with no task undone.

"'For I am already being poured out like a drink offering, and the time has come for my departure. I have fought the good fight, I have finished the race, I have kept the faith. Now there is in store for me the crown of righteousness, which the Lord, the righteous Judge, will award to me on the day — and not only to me, but also to all who have longed for his appearing.' (2 Timothy 4:6-8)

"Good-bye, Uncle Frank. Your nephew, Bruce."

There is a change happening within Bruce. It is a growth in his spirituality. It is seen in the way he lives his life, the way he talks about eternal life, the way he has allowed his love to be more obvious. He has always been a loving and devoted son that desired the unity of the family. Each day he draws closer to understanding the things he longs for are provided by the bonding love of God.

Michael displayed the greatest interest in pursuing spiritual growth. From an early age, he demonstrated interest in and thirst for spiritual knowledge. One Sunday morning Michael attended mass with other young children in a group and we were not with him at that service. When communion was given, he went forward to receive it although he had not been through instructions for receiving the sacrament. After learning about this from his grandmother, we asked him why he went to the altar for communion. He replied, "I just want to have Jesus in me!" Even at that early age, he had a better understanding of the importance of the event than many adults. Many of our family members predicted that Michael would become a priest.

While at the Naval Academy, Michael continued his quest for spiritual growth. He attended intense Bible study classes and took instruction for administering holy communion. Frequently we would attend mass at the Naval Academy Chapel. It was a way of being closer to Michael. On Mother's Day in 1981, we went to mass there, and Yvonne will never forget that day. As we got up to take communion, we were surprised to see that Michael was serving. Yvonne approached him with tear-filled eyes. These were tears of happiness and pride. Her eyes still fill with tears each time she recalls the day.

A few months after graduation, Michael's best friend was killed in a motorcycle accident. Michael suddenly drifted away from the church; he lost interest in studying the Bible; he withdrew into himself. We noticed that he became more cynical about life in general. He didn't seem to be the same happy self that had brought joy with every conversation. It was obvious that he was in a state of depression and it was becoming more difficult to talk with him. This went on for several years. He put strain on himself, his marriage, his career, and his family who cared for him so. We didn't know how to help, nor did we realize how serious the problem was.

Somehow though, Michael came out of this. I suspect that it was a matter of being more involved with his son as the growing boy required more attention from his father. The sudden change away from spiritual growth saw a reversal just as sudden toward renewed spiritual growth. The change of the past brought an even more pronounced change in the present. Michael is active in many church activities, he reads and studies the Bible often, he is active in various Christian movements, such as the Gideons and the Promise Keepers. Joy and happiness fill his life and the signs of depression are long gone. This is not to say that Michael has forgotten what caused that change, but only to say that he has grown because of the change.

Stephanie has always been what many call a free spirit. She has had many trials and tribulations, and some of these are briefly discussed in previous chapters of this book. Of her, I would say that she never showed outward signs of spiritual growth until about mid-way through her pregnancy. And it has only been in the past few months that she has been willing to talk about it.

She has said, "You just can not possibly understand the barrier guilt can be to having what I would call the good life. I don't know what repentance really means, but I know I had to admit to myself, and then to God, what I did that was wrong. Then I had to commit to change what I was doing to avoid falling into the same trap again. I didn't know how to tell God that I was sorry. The funny thing is that I believe I was always sorry for doing something I knew was wrong, but even in being sorry I wasn't able to face up to the fact that it was my own doing and I could change. Instead I got mad at anyone who even reminded me of my wrongdoing. Now I know the change that was required was to reach out to God. There is nothing I can do to free myself from this guilt. All that needs to be done has already been done for me in the sacrifice of Jesus. The changes taking place within me are directed by Him."

Throughout the Bible, both Old and New Testament, we are told to repent. This is done in our daily communication with God. But repentance is not just a mere sorrow for sins, it requires a real change in your life. It is necessary to talk over your wrong-doing with the Lord so that He can reveal to you how that change is possible. Lay your sin at the foot of the cross and He will lighten your burden; He will give you the strength to change; He will show you the way. Come to Him with a willing heart: willingly let go of the sinful way, willingly turn your life over to Him, willingly let Jesus have control of your life.

The following table presents the elements of repenting:

Steps to Repentance

"He who conceals his sins does not prosper, but whoever confesses and renounces them finds mercy." Proverbs 28:13

Step	Comment	Reference	Text
Contrition	Sorrow for offense to God	Joel 2:13	Rend your heart and not your garments. Return to the Lord your God, for he is gracious and compassionate, slow to anger and abounding in love, and he relents from sending calamity.
Confession	Confess sin to God and also to others	1 John 1:9	If we confess our sins, he is faithful and just and will forgive us our sins and purify us from all unrighteousness.
Change	Amendment to life from sinful ways	1 Peter 2:25	For you were like sheep going astray, but now you have returned to the Shepherd and Overseer of your souls.

One must be truly sorry for committing the sin, and then make an honest and open confession with God. To confess our sin to God, one must first confess it to themselves. As difficult as it may be, a confession to someone else is a significant step in removing the guilt complex from the wrongdoing. This someone else may be an interested party, i.e., companion, friend, cleric, or even the person to whom the wrongdoing was committed against. Following the confession, is a commitment to change from the ways of the wrongdoing.

"If my people, who are called by my name, will humble them-selves and pray and seek my face and turn from their wicked ways, then will I hear from heaven and will forgive their sin and will heal their land." (2 Chronicles 7:14)

Milestone #36

Confess your sins in sorrow, and change your ways.

1. Read Matthew 3:1-12. What is the message of repentance (v. 1-4)? What is the evidence of repentance (v. 5-6)? What is the illusion of repentance (v. 7-10)? What is the blessing of repentance (v. 11-12)?

2. What does repentance mean to you? Have you had an opportunity to repent? What did you do? How did you feel?

3. Do you know someone sharing the message of repentance? How was that demonstrated? Can you share an example from your personal life?

4. What are the principles of repentance which were practiced in the following verses?

    Jonah 3:5-9
    Luke 7:37-48
    Luke 15:17-21
    Acts 19:18

5. What is the relationship between repentance and the Kingdom of Heaven?

6. How would you define the central message of repentance? How will you practice repentance this week? Are you living God's power today (Acts 1:8)?

The Righteous Life

I have early childhood recollections of being taken to church each Sunday morning. It was an event. My Mother would put on her best dress, always accompanied by a wide brim hat. On our walk home after the service, we stopped at the homes of friends for a brief visit. While my Mother enjoyed the conversation, I enjoyed the pastries and milk. For that was my reward for being polite and pleasantly responding to the "good little boy" comments.

We moved from the center city of Baltimore to a southern suburb. My Mother then started me in a mission Sunday School sponsored by a local church. It was there that, at the age of twelve, I met a minister that had a marked influence on my early spiritual development. I became involved in every activity offered by that local church. As I matured, I became involved in teaching Sunday School, working on various church committees, being elected to the church council, serving as lay president and deacon of the church. I was doing all the things that I thought would make me a good person. I didn't realize then that a good person does such things because they want to serve others. It is not a matter of doing them to demonstrate that you are a good person.

Somewhere around this time, a very good friend told me that I was the most Christian person he knew. That made me feel good. Obviously this friend was an intellect and a good judge of character. Or had I just fooled him as I was fooling myself. Oh, I had the outward appearances of a good Christian. I was doing the acts of a good Christian. But something was missing.

When I got back to reading the Bible on a regular basis, I came across a verse in Luke (12:49) where the Lord says, "I have come to bring fire on the earth, and how I wish it were already kindled." I then realized what was previously missing. It was as though Jesus was talking directly to me and asking, "Where is the fire in your faith?" You see, I had become like the church in Laodicea (Revelations 3:16): neither hot nor cold, but rather lukewarm. My self-reliance had poured water on the fire of my faith. A change in me was needed.

Being active in Christian type efforts certainly is a symptom of righteous living. I knew the teaching of James from an early age, "As the body without the spirit is dead, so faith without deeds is dead." (James 2:26). But the actions cannot say what is in the heart. The motivating force within you determines the level of righteousness. It is not doing things by rote, but rather doing them by a loving desire filled with willingness and enthusiasm. It is God's will and Jesus' command that we love others and happily serve them.

I now approach opportunities to serve others with a different perspective. The tasks are no longer done with a sense of doing because it is the right thing to do. My actions are now done with a sincere desire to serve someone else and in some small way bring glory to God. I am still learning how to do this in a consistent manner. Am I living the righteous life? Let's just say that that I am attempting to do it better each and every day.

The following table provides some of my views as to what I see as good examples of the righteous life and how we can positively respond in our service to God and to others:

Acts of Righteousness

"The eyes of the Lord are on the righteous and his ears are attentive to their cry." (Psalm 34:15)

Being Righteous	Example	Response
Receive the fruit	"Like your name, O God, your praise reaches to the ends of the earth; your right hand is filled with righteousness." (Psalm 48:10)	"And this is my prayer: that your love may abound more and more in knowledge and depth of insight, so that you may be able to discern what is best and may be pure and blameless until the day of Christ, filled with the fruit of righteousness that comes through Jesus Christ -- to the glory and praise of God." (Philippians 1:9-11)
Follow the laws	"Righteous are you, O Lord, and your laws are right. The statutes you have laid down are righteous; they are fully trustworthy." (Psalm 119:137-138)	"For I tell you that unless your righteousness surpasses that of the Pharisees and the teachers of the law, you will certainly not enter the kingdom of heaven." (Matthew 5:20)
Put on the armament	"Righteousness will be his belt and faithfulness the sash around his waist." (Isaiah 11:5)	"Stand firm then, with the belt of truth buckled around your waist, with the breastplate of righteousness in place, and with your feet fitted with the readiness that comes from the gospel of peace." (Ephesians 6:14-15)
Fight the good fight	"I, the Lord, have called you in righteousness; I will take hold of your heart. I will keep you and will make you to be a covenant for the people and a light for the Gentiles." (Isaiah 42:6)	"Fight the good fight of faith. Take hold of the eternal life to which you were called when you made your good confession in the presence of many witnesses." (1 Timothy 6:11-12)
Answer all	"You answer us with awesome deeds of righteousness, O God our Savior, the hope of all the ends of the earth and of the farthest seas." (Psalm 65:5)	"You love righteousness and hate wickedness; therefore God, your God, has set you above your companions by anointing you with the oil of joy." (Psalm 45:7)

From a state of righteousness we serve others. This service is:
a.) Christlike — John 13:14; b.) Exemplifies Christian principles — Luke 10:36-37; c.) A mark of greatness — Mark
10:43-44; and d.) A universal duty — Galations 6:2.

Righteousness is a state of being given to us as a gift from God.
The righteous life is reflecting that righteousness, to God's glory,
in all we do. The emphasis I would make is that a righteous life
is filled with service to others. The joy in giving that service is
magnified by the joy one has in knowing they are pleasing God.

There is a passage in the Bible that caused me to reflect on how
to live the righteous life. "All the Israelite men and women who
were willing brought to the Lord freewill offerings for all the
work the Lord through Moses had commanded them to do."
(Exodus 35:29) To me the words, "All...who were willing,"
reflects a willing attitude in coming to the Lord.
"Brought...freewill offerings," states that the will must result in
some action. "For all the work," infers accomplishments. In
summary, Attitude leads to Action which results in Accomplishments.

Milestone #37

Live the righteous life.

1. What does being righteous mean to you? What actions are necessary? What attitudes are necessary?

2. What does service to others mean to you? Service to God? How do you serve others? How do you serve God?

3. Do acts of kindness and service reflect the righteousness of an individual? Explain. What could be the motivators for providing acts of kindness and service? What should be the motivators?

4. Do you recall any opportunities to serve others that you have not responded to? If so, why? Do you feel that you have an awareness to serve others? Why?

5. What Christian principles are exemplified in leading a righteous life?

6. Do you feel you live the righteous life? How is this evident to you? To others? What can you do to lead a more righteous life?

Here I Am

What an inspiring night! In fact, it had been an emotional and inspiring week. Several hundred people have made it possible for thousands of others to get to know Christ better. The event was called "Mainline '89". It was an evangelistic/renewal crusade put on by the John Guest Evangelistic Team. More than one hundred area churches sponsored the crusade. But this warm July evening was the final night. There was much joy in being at the Devon Horse Show Grounds for these past eight nights. Now the realization that this successful crusade was coming to an end began to set in. The joy was mixed with sadness. It was like a visit with a special friend was ending.

I had seen parts of many crusades on television. Never did I experience from those watchings the feelings that I had during this event. It must have been the fact that I was participating. That in itself was something, for I could not possibly have previously considered going to a crusade evangelism for eight consecutive nights. For me, evangelism always carried a label of fanatic with it. But again, my only real, in person, experience was as a youth going to some revival meetings. But this was all so very different. In reality, I had been involved for six months in preparation for this one week event.

One year before I had an awakening of my spirituality. My thirst for Bible study grew. Yvonne and I were sharing the meaning of our faith with each other every day. We were going to Bible study classes together each week. In my personal renewal and enthusiasm, I began wondering how I could share my faith with others. Then one November day we received a notice in the mail about the coming crusade. It was like a personal invitation from God to go do some work for him. I made contact with the local organizing committee and became involved in the committee efforts necessary to make the event successful.

As the time drew nearer, I had the desire to do more. The promotional materials indicated that one of the related activities would be a series of classes conducted in April on confident Christian living. Yvonne and I agreed that this was just the thing. As we attended those classes, we learned that completion of the classes qualified you to be considered as a counselor at the crusade. I inquired as to what that really meant, and was advised that a counselor would be assigned to specific individuals that came forth during the crusade to seek conversion to, or renewal in, the Christian faith. Now this was an opportunity to share with a stranger what my faith meant to me. Was I really prepared to do this? Even with that question in the back of my mind, I committed to being a counselor during the crusade.

The time was now here. On a Saturday evening in late-June we had a warm-up meeting on the show grounds. Hundreds of workers and their friends and families were there. I could feel the emotion swell within my body as we prayerfully prepared for the opening day. I prayed intently that God would direct me in doing His work. The next evening I went with great anticipation and considerable doubt about my readiness. It was more beautiful and inspiring than I imagined. The capacity crowd was stirred by the music and the oratory presentations. Then at the close of the ceremonies, hundreds of people came out of the stands to the center of the arena to commit to Jesus. Now it was time to see if I was really ready to share my faith with others.

Each evening I had the good fortune of counseling two or three of the individuals that came forth to the arena area. And each evening I had the reward of being God's instrument in helping someone else learn more about Jesus. I believe I received more than I gave. Following the crusade, I had the opportunity of following up with those individuals to nurture their spiritual growth. In that nurturing, I nurtured my own growth. God indeed was at work in all of us. That experience has given me the confidence to share my faith with others in many ways. This was made possible by willingly letting God direct my steps. All

I had to do was say, "Here I am, Lord."

There are many references in the Bible of people who have been ready to serve. The following table reflects the instances when someone responded to God's call with a willing attitude. It is a challenge for all of us.

Ready to Serve

"Then I said, 'Here I am, I have come -- it is written about me in the scroll. I desire to do your will, O my God, your law is within my heart." (Psalm 40:7-8)

Servant	Reference	Text
Abraham	Genesis 22:11	But the angel of the Lord called out from heaven, "Abraham! Abraham!" "Here I am," he replied.
Jacob	Genesis 46:2	And God spoke to Israel in a vision at night and said, "Jacob! Jacob!" "Here I am," he replied.
Moses	Exodus 3:4	When the Lord saw that he had gone over to look, God called to him from within the bush, "Moses! Moses!" And Moses said, "Here I am."
Samuel	1 Samuel 3:4	Then the Lord called Samuel. Samuel answered, "Here I am."
Jesus	Matthew 26:42	My Father, if it is not possible for this cup to be taken away unless I drink from it, may your will be done.
Everyone	1 John 2:17	The world and its desires pass away, but the man who does the will of God lives forever.

It is easy to know God's will. You must be constantly ready to say, "Here I am, Lord." As you take a step toward God with a willing heart, He leads the way and opens opportunities for you. As you do God's will, you will experience the wonderful joy of knowing you are bringing glory to His name. You will indeed feel closer to God.

Each singing of the refrain from the hymn, "Here I Am, Lord," brings a renewed desire to serve the Lord with all my heart.

Here I am, Lord. Is it I, Lord?
I have heard You calling in the night.
I will go, Lord, if You lead me,
I will hold your people in my heart.

Milestone #38

Be ready to serve the Lord.

1. Where are some of the places in this world that you have found the most fascinating to visit? Have you been there? Why did you go? What is the one place in the world that you would never want to go? Would you go if God called you?

2. Do you know of anyone that truly believes that God has called them to a special service? How did they know they were called? Do you feel you have been called to a special service? How?

3. What is your work? Do you believe your work matters to God? Why? How can you serve God through your work?

4. How can we know what God is calling us to do (Joshua 1:8-9)? Have you heard the call? How have you responded?

5. Who is responsible for fulfilling the mission of the true call from God (1 Thessalonians 5:24)? What are some ways we can be responsive to the commands of Jesus (Matthew 28:19-20)?

6. Are you ready to serve the Lord? How will you serve Him this week in the family? At work? In the community? In the church?

Death

Readiness

"Code Blue! Code Blue!" The announcement over the loud speaker brings a sense of urgency throughout the hospital. A specialized team rushes to the announced area to begin a frantic effort to save a life. Even those not directly involved are frozen in place for a moment as they contemplate the seriousness of the situation. I will never forget the call I got in the middle of the night advising me that Yvonne had just gone through a Code Blue experience. Rushing to the hospital, I realized that the telephone call had the same chilling affects that the unexpected announcement in the hospital would have. This was compounded by the fact that someone I loved dearly was involved.

One morning in 1989, Yvonne could not get out of bed. She had severe back pain and was almost completely immobilized from the intensity of the pain. We are fortunate to have a family doctor that is willing to make house calls. He came and gave Yvonne some pain medication so she could rest, and he advised that she needed to see a neurologist as soon as possible. After the necessary tests were made and two confirming opinions were obtained, Yvonne agreed to have the necessary surgery to relieve the condition caused by the herniated disc between the fourth and fifth vertebrae in the lumbar region.

Following surgery, Yvonne was in great discomfort and required some sleeping medication to enable her to rest. She was given a sleeping pill, and we were not aware of the side effects that often result from taking this particular drug. As the drug took effect, Yvonne began to feel an uneasy change take place within her body. She began talking with God. Thoughts of her life flashed through her mind and she raced forward in time to review the things that she felt had to be done. Her last conscious comment was to Jesus as she cried out, "I want to know you more!" There was a sudden need within her to know more about Jesus and His teachings. She wanted to become more Christlike and desired more time to learn how.

Her next recollection was abruptly waking up and reaching toward a vague image of someone at the foot of her bed. She sensed it was a dear friend that had recently died after a long illness with cancer. No words were being spoken, yet they were communicating. Yvonne understood that her dear friend was at peace in a beautiful and joyful environment. She got out of bed and walked across the room thinking of all the things that she was leaving undone, and she thought to herself, "I am not ready to go, but if it is Your will then let it be."

Suddenly, Yvonne felt that she was about to pass out. She was near the bathroom and she was able to reach in and press the nurse call button. She awoke as four people were carrying her back to her bed. A light gray cloud seemed to be filling the room. She had no pain, no discomfort. Sometime later she awoke in bed; a nurse advised her that they almost lost her. The nurse said she had found her and called for the Code Blue; she comforted her and told Yvonne she would be back to check-in on her. It was after that I received the call. The nurse came back in the morning and reassured Yvonne that she was doing fine. Yvonne never saw that nurse again during her nine day stay in the hospital.

In looking back at the incident, Yvonne thought, at the time, that she must have some significant tasks to do before she was worthy of being in God's presence. Now she sees that it is in the day-to-day activities in helping others that she is serving her Lord. These daily efforts now take on a very different meaning. That meaning brings new enthusiasm to caring for family and friends. The menial tasks of today are in a small way serving others. This matters to God. By serving others, one serves God. By serving God, one readies themselves for being in His presence.

What I see in this experience is the readiness of the Code Blue
Team as it prepares to help someone else. I see Yvonne's perspective of not being ready enough to be in God's presence, but
still being submissive to God's will. Were the recollections of
Yvonne only drug induced imaginings? Did she have what could
be termed a near-death experience? The reality of the situation is
that Yvonne had an awareness of needing to do more to be
worthy of being with God. Her state of readiness was not
complete, in contrast to the Code Blue Team whose state of
readiness was complete.

We must get ourselves to readiness for the day will come when
we will not have another chance. The so called Age of Enlight-
enment that began in the latter part of the nineteenth century,
avoided any discussion about death and sin and hell. That legacy
has carried into our own generation as we continue to avoid such
discussions. I am not suggesting that we concentrate on the fire
and brimstone messages that some evangelists are so good at
delivering. But I am suggesting that a fact of our earthly existence is death and we should live each day in preparation for the
last day on earth.

Be Ready

"Watch and pray so that you will not fall into temptation. The spirit is willing, but the body in weak." (Matthew 26:41)

Condition	Reference	Text
Stand firm A way is provided	1 Corinthians 10:12-13	So, if you think you are standing firm, be careful that you don't fall. No temptation has seized you except what is common to man. And God is faithful; he will not let you be tempted beyond what you can bear. But when you are tempted, he will also provide a way out so that you can stand up under it.
Walk in the light Be alert and self-controlled	1 Thessalonians 5:5-6	You are all sons of the light and sons of the day. We do not belong to the night or the darkness. So then, let us not be like others, who are asleep, but let us be alert and self-controlled.
Wake up Serve	Revelations 3:2-3	Wake up! Strengthen what remains and is about to die, for I have not found your deeds complete in the sight of God. Remember, therefore, what you have received and heard; obey it, and repent. But if you do not wake up, I will come like a thief, and you will not know at what time I will come to you.

The ancient Egyptian pharaohs prepared for their earthly death, by constructing large monuments to house all their possessions that they felt were required for going into the next life. Gold, tools, pets and even people were entombed with the pharaoh to ready the monarch for the trip to the afterlife. As we know, this is a journey that you take on your own. You cannot take your possessions with you. These possessions do not measure your readiness.

Some time ago I read a newspaper article about a man that prepared for his funeral. He picked out his coffin and slept in it; he rode in the hearse he selected for the occasion; he wrote his obituary; he rehearsed the funeral service. This is perhaps the extreme for those who give no consideration to death at all. But it does not come close to measuring the readiness of someone for death.

Yvonne's younger brother, Frank, has, for several years, said that he was ready to meet his Lord. He spoke confidently about making every attempt to be Christlike, and he was excited about the possibility of being in the awesome presence of God. One could sense the attitude of happiness and excitement that was in him when he spoke of such things. Was he ready? He believed he was. Only God knows. Yvonne's brother recently was taken from us as a result of a sudden, massive heart attack. We grieve his absence, but rejoice in knowing that he has gone on to an awaited fellowship with the Lord.

I was asked to share in the giving of the eulogy for Frank. As I prepared, the most outstanding trait that came to mind was service. Service to God, service to country, service to family. Without question Frank had a sincere and strong faith in God and in Jesus Christ. It provided the framework for his high moral standards and unquestionable righteous conduct. He was always ready to help someone. No effort was too difficult, and it was always done with a willing heart, a helping hand and a smiling face.

I remember a young man that graduated from boot camp and inspired our son to dream of becoming like his Uncle Frank. He provided the model of a good Marine, and encouraged Michael in his military career. I remember the seasoned soldier returning from Vietnam. He didn't want to talk about what he did there, but I know with confidence, he did whatever was asked of him. I remember the tough drill instructor who barked orders to big, strong men and could also talk soothingly to his plants to nurture their growth. His gruff exterior hid a gentle man who respected and cared for all life. This gentle warrior served his country well.

I remember a devoted family member that provided for his mother. He extended his family to include a large circle of friends and he worked unselfishly hard at serving them all. As our son, Bruce, stated, "Uncle Frank was never too busy to have time for a long walk in the woods, and to listen and quietly teach while a young boy worked out how to become a man." He has touched my life and given me many wonderful memories. In his service to all, he served God. Was Frank ready? I believe he was.

Milestone #39

Be always ready to meet your Lord.

1. Enoch was the great grandfather of Noah, and Elijah was a significant Old Testament prophet. These men seemed to have had unusual deaths (Genesis 5:24, Hebrew 11:5, 2 Kings 2:11). What is similar and significant about the death of these men? What does it indicate of their readiness to die?

2. Do you know of anyone who had prepared for their physical death? What preparation did they make? Why were those preparations necessary?

3. Have you been directly involved in discussions with someone about their death and their preparations for it? How did you, would you, feel having these discussions with a friend? A family member? Do you feel this person was truly ready to die?

4. What do you have to do to be prepared for death? Do you have insurance? A will? A living will? How prepared are you to die? Have you talked with your family about the possibility of death of yourself or any family member? Was it a difficult conversation? Why?

5. What do you believe it means to "meet your maker"? Is there any preparation required for this? Explain. Do you believe people are generally ready to accept the eventuality of death? Explain.

6. Do you believe you are ready to die? Explain. What do you need to do to be ready?

Penalty or Reward

It had been a near perfect pregnancy. Yvonne had little trouble over the last nine months in carrying the anxiously awaited child within her. Just the week before the doctor advised Yvonne that all was well. I had much concern about Yvonne because her doctors advised that she should not have any more children. They said her health was too delicate to chance the rigors of childbirth again. But she had done well. The baby had a strong heart beat and was very active. The child could be born at any time now. It was already three weeks past the expected delivery date. Both the child and mother were in strong health.

Then during the night, Yvonne awoke me. It wasn't the message I was expecting to receive. She simply said, "Our child is dead."

"But how can that be? How do you know that?", I responded.

Yvonne said, "I just know. About a half hour ago I woke up and knew something was wrong. I have been lying here waiting for our baby to make some movement, but it is still. I have been asking myself what I did wrong. This child would so make our family complete. Something within me says that all will be okay. I don't know what that means, but I do feel better now than I did a few minutes ago."

Yvonne was scheduled for a routine doctor visit the next day. During that visit it was confirmed that the baby within her did indeed die for there was no heart beat or movement. The doctor advised that she should deliver the child naturally and not have it removed surgically. It was another three days before the child was delivered. Each day grew more difficult for Yvonne. The great happiness that we all felt had turned into sadness. It must be all the more painful for the mother.

When the delivery finally occurred, the doctor came into the waiting room and advised me that our baby boy had made a loop

in the umbilical cord and passed through it. As the active child
moved about it drew the knot increasingly tighter until all
nourishment to the unborn infant was cut off. The doctor said
that there was no way of determining this difficulty before birth.
It was but an unusual accident in childbirth.

Yvonne and I searched for answers as to why this should happen.
We discussed the possibility of having done something wrong
and this was our punishment. But we could not accept that as an
act of a merciful God. Certainly the child could not have done
anything wrong before entering the world. The pain of the loss
could not be relieved.

Some nights I would see Yvonne standing at the doorway of the
bedrooms of our two healthy sons. She just looked lovingly at
them. No words needed to be spoken. I knew she was looking
for our third son, and wondering how he would compare to his
brothers.

Several months after the incident Yvonne asked if I would
consider adopting a child. My response was that we could
pursue it, but I knew it was difficult to obtain an infant. We had
gotten our sons a puppy to fill the void caused by the loss of a
baby brother. Now we were ready to address the void that we
felt as parents. I must truly say, that I was willing to do this for
Yvonne. We knew that it was too dangerous for Yvonne to
consider conceiving again. It seemed to be our best alternative.
Now that it is all behind us, I am so glad that we did.

It has been thirty years since that still-birth incident. Yvonne is
still looking for the son that was lost. She knows that she will
see him when she joins him in God's heavenly kingdom. But the
search within her heart and mind continues. We learned that the
emptiness caused by the absence of someone cannot be filled by
someone else. Each person crafts a unique position within your
heart. Your heart can expand to accept someone else, but the
void of the other remains.

We do not believe that there was any penalty involved in the taking of our third son. No penalty to us; certainly no penalty to him. Without that loss we would not have adopted a child. Certainly that was rewarding, but not a reward for the loss. Our third son is surely in the heavenly kingdom, but that is by the grace of God and not a reward from having come into this world. This event was the will of God. The reason to us remains a mystery. In His time we will understand.

In this earthly life, we measure everything by contrast. We can say that bad judges good. That is to say, if we define bad and what is being measured doesn't fit that definition, then it is good, or vice versa. Bad gives meaning to good. And so in death, we have an opportunity to know the meaning of life.

The Death Judgment

"For if, by the trespass of the one man, death reigned through that one man, how much more will those who receive God's abundant provision of grace and of the gift of righteousness reign in life through the one man, Jesus Christ." (Romans 5:17)

Topic	Penalty	Reward
Warning	But you must not eat from the tree of the knowledge of good and evil, for when you eat of it you will surely die. (Genesis 2:17)	The senseless man does not know, fools do not understand, that though the wicked spring up like grass and all evildoers flourish, they will be forever destroyed. (Psalm 92:6-7)
Cause	Therefore just as sin entered the world through one man, and death through sin, and in this way death came to all men, because all sinned (Ro. 5:12)	For the wages of sin are death, but the gift of God is eternal life in Christ Jesus our Lord. (Romans 6:23)
Result	To Adam he said, 'Because you listened to your wife and ate from the tree about which I commanded you, 'You must not eat of it,' cursed is the ground because of you; through painful toil you will eat of it all the days of your life. (Genesis 3:17)	But now he has reconciled you by Christ's physical body through death to present you holy in his sight, without blemish and free from accusation. (Colossians 1:22)
Universality	I know you will bring me down to death, to the place appointed for all the living. (Job 30:23)	And he died for all, that those who live should no longer live for themselves but for him who died for them and was raised again. (2 Corinthians 5:15)
Progression	Then, after desire has conceived, it gives birth to sin; and sin, when it is full-grown, gives birth to death. (James 1:15)	Not only so, but we rejoice in our sufferings, because we know that suffering produces perseverance; perseverance, character; character, hope. (Ro.5:3-4)
Ownership	The soul who sins is the one who will die. The son will not share the guilt of the father, nor will the father share the guilt of the son. The righteousness of the righteous man will be credited to him, and the wickedness of the wicked will be charge against him. (Ezekiel 18:20)	Remember this: Whoever turns a sinner from the error of his way will save him from death and cover over a multitude of sins. (James 5:20)

There is indeed suffering in this world. And suffering is so often looked upon as a penalty situation as many will look at death in this way. "We are hard pressed on every side, but not crushed; perplexed, but not in despair; persecuted, but not abandoned; struck down, but not destroyed. We always carry around in us the death of Jesus, so that the life of Jesus may also be revealed in our body." (2 Corinthians 4:8-10) It is enough for me to know that God's will is at work.

I cannot give answers to the difficult questions people ask about their suffering, or the death of their loved ones. God holds the answers to these questions. I do know that God is just, and a heavenly reward awaits the righteous. God is also merciful, and provides everyone with the opportunity to share in the ultimate reward. The innocent child, the reformed sinner, the righteous person all have a place in the heavenly kingdom. Through the life and death of Jesus, each of us can now face the certain death and the life that comes from that certainty.

Milestone #40

Face the certainty of death with the certainty of eternal life.

1. Why is there death? Is death a penalty? If so, to whom and why? If not, can it be a reward? Explain.

2. An infant dies. Is this a penalty or reward? Explain. Is this any different for a 90 year-old grandparent dying? Explain.

3. Why is there suffering in this world? Do you believe God has a purpose in allowing such suffering? Explain. Do you believe righteous people have suffering? Why?

4. Do you agree that bad judges good? Explain. Ugly judges beauty? Explain. Death judges life? Explain.

5. Have you considered the impact your death would have on others? What impact do you see on Family? Friends? Co-workers? Others? How have you prepared yourself for that impact?

6. Would you consider your death a penalty or reward? Explain. Could you change your view of this? How?

Letting Go

The loss of someone you hold dear is most difficult. Whether death comes slowly as in a long, extended illness or suddenly as in an accident, the impact is much the same. An overwhelming emptiness occurs within the loved ones of the departed. To fill that emptiness many will busy themselves with their work or household chores to keep from dwelling on the grief of not having their loved one with them. Others will go into a long period of despair and allow their grief to deepen. Whatever course is taken, memories of the departed will steadily flash through your mind as well as thoughts of all the things that should have been said or done. Just as the departed one had to let go of this worldly life, so do the remaining loved ones need to let go of the sadness and despair that grasps them so tightly.

It seems to me that in anyone's life they can only count a very few select people that are considered to be best friends. We all have many acquaintances that enter and exit our life, but only a limited number become so close to us that we can share most everything with them. I have been fortunate in that I had never really lost a truly best friend until last year. Even though it was late in life, it still brought the deep feeling of emptiness. To me the illness had seemed so brief, although the doctors said that the cancer was active within my friend, Jim, for sometime. Once admitted to the hospital, the tests revealed that any surgery would only somewhat delay the inevitable and would most likely have unpleasant side effects. Jim busied himself at putting things in order so that his dear wife would not be burdened with any financial matters after his death. Within a few weeks, he knew he had done all that could be done. He and his wife agreed, it was now okay to stop the struggle, to stop the suffer-ing, to find the peace. Quietly he stopped the fight and let go of this world to reach out to the next life.

I wrote a brief note to my friend. It was a message late sent, a message not read, a message known by Jim. "This brief note is to let you know that my thoughts and prayers are with you, my dear friend. In my advancing maturity, I reflect on times long since passed. You are frequently a part of my fond memories. I want you to know also that I consider myself blessed because you have touched my life. In this time of need, I wish so that I could help you carry your burden. But I know that someone stronger than I is there with you. May Jesus' healing presence forever remain with you...."

For forty years we had shared in each others joys and triumphs, sadness and hardships. Often, we would be parted by distance and time, but never were we parted in our love for each other as true friends. Each time we were united, it was as though we had never been apart. Space and time melted away. And so it will be the next time we are united.

Some years before this, our younger son, Michael, experienced the loss of two dear friends. Michael and Cheryl had been married less than a year. The gala events of the Naval Academy graduation and wedding were still very fresh in everyone's memory. Michael selected his childhood friend, Bert, to be an usher and attendant at the wedding. Bert took the responsibility seriously and contributed much to the happiness of the occasion. Then, suddenly, an unfortunate motorcycle accident took the life of this young man.

This tragedy had quite an impact on Michael. The happy memories of the wedding were now overcome with the grieving for the loss of a friend. Michael has recently said, "It was like the loss of a brother, a part of me was gone." We noticed an immediate change in Michael. He avoided doing all the things that Bert and he would do together. He was depressed, and he didn't call home as often. He left nuclear sub school in Florida to make the trip to Maryland and attend the funeral services. Absence from the intense studies and his state of depression lowered his class standings. We were very concerned. A few weeks later we received a letter from Michael containing the following:

"In the past few months, I've learned many things in school but none seem as important as what I've learned about myself. The world has been an incredible teacher. One of the things I've learned about is my own mortality. Bert's death left me without a friend of a lifetime. I know that I could never again have a friend as close as he was. In his death, many secrets about ourselves died. No one else knows some of the things Bert took to the grave. Those things seem trivial compared to the words left unsaid; those things that should have been said but never were because of one reason or another. These are the things that tear at me daily. Those simple words, thoughts and feelings hound me constantly. I can do nothing but hope he knew, as I do, what our friendship meant to each other. I know to what depth he touched my life; I hope he knows too. It is these thoughts which prompt this writing. The words that have to be said before we are sorry that we never did...

"I love the strength of our family. We all contribute to it. The family has come to my rescue through my times of trouble. Thank you for that. I love you all more than life itself. I want you all to know how much I do love you. I think of you daily. I couldn't say that to Bert. But I've now said it to all of you. Should death ever separate us before I can say it again, remember I loved you more than anything in the world and will be with you always."

From this letter, Michael's recovery began. He let go of Bert and replaced it with a more outgoing show of his love for the entire family. Before he could fully recover though, tragedy struck again. Michael's roommate at the Academy, Bill, died in an airplane crash.

Bill had gone into the Navy Air program and was in the midst of making a decision as to whether to go into Top Gun training or join the Navy's Blue Angels. Michael was fishing in the James River in Virginia and noticed a jet making some practice runs for some demonstration. A little later he saw what seemed to be a column of black smoke rising somewhere down the coast. His first thought was that his friend Bill had crashed. Immediately he headed for shore, and the call he didn't want to come was received by him a few hours later.

Michael had a bit of a different reaction to this loss. There was the same sense of avoidance he had before. But now he seemed to be numb. He couldn't, or wouldn't, cry. The repairing that was going on in his own life was suspended. But Michael then reached out to Bill's parents and tried all he could do to comfort them. He let go of Bill so he could try to grasp his parents and help them heal their pain. The friendship he had with Bill has been transferred to his parents. In some way, I believe it helped the healing in all of them.

Letting go is not easy. For the one that must let go of this world, the instinct is to fight for survival. The intensity of the fight is stronger in some than in others. For those left behind, the instinct is to grieve all the more intently as if that grieving changes what has been and what could have been. To keep it in perspective, the hope of eternal peace and happiness that comes with being in the presence of God must be held close to your heart.

One must look to the life that comes from death. As the caterpillar gives way to the beautiful butterfly, so death gives way to a new, eternal life. In each loss we experience, there is a new experience before us that would not have been known without the loss. We are not to forget that which is lost, but rather learn from memories of having and the lessons of the grief. This earthly experience is to prepare us for the eternal existence before our God.

Life through Death

"For to me, to live is Christ and to die is gain." (Philippians 1:21)

Topic	Reference	Text
Time of death not known	Ecclesiates 8:7-8	Since no man knows the future, who can tell what is to come? No man has power over the wind to contain it; so no one has power over the day of his death.
Burdened in earthly dwelling	2 Corinthians 5:1,4	Now we know that if the earthly tent we live in is destroyed, we have a building from God, an eternal house in heaven, not built by human hands....For while we are in this tent, we groan and are burdened, because we do not wish to be unclothed but to be clothed with our heavenly dwelling, so that what is mortal may be swallowed up by life.
Death brings life	John 12:24	I tell you the truth, unless a kernel of wheat falls to the ground and dies, it remains only a single seed. But if it dies, it produces many seeds.
Opportunity for all	2 Samuel 14:14	Like water spilled on the ground, which cannot be recovered, so we must die. But God does not take away life; instead, he devises ways so that a banished person may not remain estranged from him.
Refuge for the righteous	Proverbs 14:32	When calamity comes, the wicked are brought down, but even in death the righteous have refuge.
Rest from labor	Revelations 14:13	Then I heard a voice from heaven say, "Write: Blessed are the dead who die in the Lord from now on." "Yes," says the Spirit, "they will rest from their labor, for their deeds will follow them."

Milestone #41

Let go of grief and despair by living in Christ.

1. Why does one mourn over the loss of someone they love?
   Have you lost a loved one? Did you mourn the loss? For
   how long? Do you feel the mourning was justified? Why?

2. Grieving the loss of a loved one can cause despair. Have you
   ever experienced that despair? What impact did it have on
   your daily life? Have you known anyone that you feel was in
   mourning for a prolonged period of time? Was that person
   the same during the grieving as before the loss? Explain.

3. What else, other than the loss of a loved one, can cause
   despair? Why? Have you experienced any of these?

4. Has anyone attempted to comfort you in a time of grief or
   despair? If so, what did they say or do? Did it help you at
   all? What would you say or do for a friend that was grieving
   or in an attitude of despair?

5. Read John 11:1-42. What does this say of Jesus' friendship
   with Lazarus? How did He comfort Martha and Mary? What
   was Martha and Mary's response to Jesus when He told them
   that Lazarus will rise again? What message do you get from
   this miraculous episode? Who does Jesus say He is?

6. Could turning off life support systems for someone in a
   hospital critical care unit be considered letting go? Explain.
   How would you define letting go in death? In despair? In
   grief? What would enable you to let go?

Jesus' Last Words

Yvonne received a call from her sobbing sister. The words were difficult for her to say. She finally blurted out, "Daddy said that he didn't want to leave us girls, but he had to go." Yvonne's sister had just left the hospital. Their father had been ill for a couple years. He had taken an early retirement and had not adjusted to it at all. Perhaps the activity of his work hid the symptoms of his illness. Or possibly, the lack of work resulted in reduced strength and lower resistance to the illness. The fact of the matter is that his health had been declining since retirement and these past few months showed an accelerated pace of deterioration.

The words spoken from his hospital bed in May 1979 were not his last. On reflection though, these words stand out in Yvonne's mind. Her father was released from the hospital and went home for a while. Yvonne recalls several other comments that her father made which closely related to what he had told her sister in the hospital. It seemed as though he was trying to get things in order in his own way. While he made no attempt to get personally involved, it appeared that he wanted others to talk about the possibility of death and to make plans accordingly. Yvonne told her mother, "Daddy knows he is dying. He is worried about all of us. Let's make him as comfortable as possible and let him know that everything is taken care of."

In August of that year, Yvonne's father died in the hospital just shortly after she left his bedside. By this time, his alert mind had drifted into another world. His statements didn't necessarily make a lot of sense to us in this world. But then words were not needed for Yvonne to know that her father loved her and wanted her to be provided for and protected. In Yvonne's heart, her father's last words were: "I love you my daughter and I will always protect you."

There are only two references in the Bible where someone has escaped the pain of death. In the Book of Genesis, Enoch, the great-grandfather of Noah, was taken directly to heaven (Genesis 5:24, Hebrews 11:5). Later the major prophet, Elijah, was taken up in a whirlwind (2 Kings 2:11). Jesus had to experience death if He was to take the place of all men and women.

The scene of the suffering and the death of Jesus has been told countless times and in countless ways. And in each telling the agony is revealed. The biblical account captures the concern that Jesus has for others, even in His own suffering. The following table reflects the recorded last words of Jesus before His death and resurrection.

Jesus Speaks from the Cross

"The Word became flesh and lived for a while among us. We have seen his glory, the glory of the one and only Son, who came from the Father, full of grace and truth." (John 1:14)

To Whom Spoken	Reference	Text
The Father	Luke 23:34	Jesus said, "Father, forgive them, for they do not know what they are doing." And they divided up his clothes by casting lots.
The criminal	Luke 23:43	Jesus answered him, "I tell you the truth, today you will be with me in paradise."
Mary and the disciple, John	John 19:26-27	When Jesus saw his mother there, and the disciple he loved standing nearby, he said to his mother, "Dear woman, here is your son," and to his disciple, "Here is your mother." From that time on, this disciple took her into his home.
The Father	Matthew 27:46	About the ninth hour Jesus cried out in a loud voice, "Eloi, Eloi, lama sabachthani?" -- which means, "My God, My God, why have you forsaken me?"
The centurion	John 19:28	Later, knowing that all was now completed, and so that the Scripture would be fulfilled, Jesus said, "I am thirsty."
The Father	Luke 23:46	Jesus called out with a loud voice, "Father, into your hands I commit my spirit." When he said this, he breathed his last.
To all	John 19:30	When he had received the drink, Jesus said, "It is finished." With that, he bowed his head and gave up his spirit.

The concern that Jesus showed for others while in great pain, reflects the ever-loving and ever-caring nature of our Savior. He asks forgiveness for all, promises salvation for the confessed criminal, cares for His mother.

At the moment Jesus cries out, "My God, My God, why have you forsaken me?", the sins of all are taken on by Him. This is the cry of human agony that was experienced by Jesus. These words are also the first words in Psalm 22. As Jesus speaks these words, perhaps He is asking all to remember the words of that Psalm. A careful reading reflects the great agony that was to occur some one thousand years later. Verse 28 of Psalm 22 mentions the dividing of the clothes by casting lots. Psalm 31 also has much familiarity with the scene at the cross. Jesus words, "Father, into your hands I commit my spirit.", can be found in verse 5 of that Psalm. This is but the continuing linkage of the Old and New Testaments.

The order of the sayings in the table are my best efforts at putting them in sequence. To me it doesn't really matter what the specific words were that He last spoke. For in my heart the last words are: "I love you. Lead your life in the example I set for you. Follow my ways and I will assure you of my eternal protection."

Milestone #42

Remember the last words of a loved one.

1. Read Psalm 22. Do you see any comparison of David's psalm to Jesus' words from the cross? Explain. What does David have to say about despair? About deliverance? About others? What does Jesus have to say from the cross about despair, if anything? About deliverance? About others?

2. Do you recall the last words a loved one said to you today? Did they have any special meaning to you? Why, or why not? Do you recall the last words anyone said to you shortly before death? What were the circumstances? What made them memorable?

3. What were the last words you said to a loved one today? Did they have special meaning to you? Were they intended to have special meaning to the loved one? Is it a communication you would want the loved one to recall? Why?

4. Read Ephesians 4:25-32. What does this tell you about communicating with others? What can you do to communicate better with loved ones?

5. Is there someone that you have not seen for awhile and you feel you must communicate with them? If so, what is the barrier to that communication? Should you make the effort to communicate? Why?

6. Identify three loved ones you feel the closest to. If you knew you would not see them, or talk to them, again, what would you tell them? Why?

Everlasting Life

Eternal Life

Many years ago, I asked my father if he believed in God. He said, "I'm not sure there is a God, but I know that believing there is one makes you a better person." That answer satisfied me. But more recently I realized that my father would not have eternal life unless he accepted Jesus as his Lord and Savior. Over a course of months we talked briefly about the subject, but he was very noncommittal in what he was accepting. Then in August 1989 he had a heart attack and was hospitalized. I rushed to Maryland to be with him as he was scheduled for some invasive test routines. I got there before he went into the tests and asked if he had been thinking about our discussions on God and if he believed in eternal life. Dad said, "I just can't imagine a place that could hold all the souls of the millions of people that have lived on this earth." I replied, "Dad, do you know how insignificant the earth is in our galaxy and how small our galaxy is in what we now define as the heavens? Don't you feel that it is possible for God to provide a heavenly home for all His children?" Dad agreed.

Dad came through the tests successfully and agreed to have the required by-pass surgery. I returned to Maryland the following week on the night before the scheduled surgery. We talked more about eternal life and the love that God has shown us through His Son. The next morning I arrived at the hospital a little before 6 a.m. to find that Dad was in the midst of a major heart attack and he was wheeled past me to the intensive care unit. After they stabilized him, I was allowed to visit with him and the doctor explained that by-pass surgery was no longer possible and a more risky procedure was the only option available. Dad and I talked again and I told him that I wanted him to invite Jesus into his heart and trust in Christ's healing presence. Dad prayed with me to receive Jesus. By being willing, God used me as His instrument to bring Dad to the truth. Dad died on the operating table, but that was overcome by his new birth into Christ's kingdom. I am thankful that God revealed Himself to Dad so that he could go into the operating room with the assurance of eternal life.

Since Dad had a tube down his throat and a lot of equipment hooked to him, I was not certain that Dad actually prayed the prayer. He was fully aware of what was going on, but he couldn't speak; he would just blink his eyes and squeeze my hand. I prayed that God would give me a sign so that I would know that Dad had achieved eternal life.

Three days later we had a burial service at the cemetery and I spoke about how the old must give way to the new, and how there must be a death before there can be new life. I mentioned that the caterpillar must give way to the butterfly. And then, a large black butterfly with gold trimmed wings flew through the family and friends gathered at the grave site. It landed on the flowers at Dad's grave and rested there. As the benediction was given, the butterfly lifted off the flowers and disappeared into the heavens. "Thank You God for my answer."

There are hundreds of references in the Bible to life after death. Terms such as salvation, resurrection, eternal life, everlasting life, gathered to his people, etc. The following table are just a few:

ETERNAL LIFE

"For God so loved the world that He gave His only Son, that whoever believes in Him shall not perish, but have eternal life." (John 3:16)

Selected Text	Reference	Comments
"Now this is eternal life; that they may know you, the only true God, and Jesus Christ, whom you sent."	John 17:3	Eternal life defined Spiritual knowledge; truth; God is truth
"And this is the testimony: God has given us eternal life, and this life is in his Son."	1 John 5:11	Gift from God Only through Christ
"....whoever is thirsty, let him come; and whoever wishes, let him take of the free gift of the water of life."	Rev. 22:17	The free gift is available. We need only to accept it. See also Isa. 55:1, Ro. 6:23
"And this is what He promised us--eternal life"	1 John 2:25	God's promise
"The Lord is not slow in keeping his promise, as some understand slowness. He is patient with you, not wanting anyone to perish...."	2 Peter 3:9	In God's time. His plan is eternal life for all
"....from infancy you have known the holy Scriptures, which are able to make you wise for salvation through faith in Christ Jesus."	2 Tim. 3:15	Bible source of true wisdom. Faith in Christ required
"I write these things to you who believe in the name of the Son of God that you may know you have eternal life."	1 John 5:13	Assurance of eternal life
"....And the glory of the Lord will be revealed and all mankind together will see it (God's salvation)."	Isaiah 40:5	All will see God's glory. See also Luke 3:6
"....everyone whose name is written in the book - will be delivered. Multitudes who sleep in the dust of the earth will awake: some to everlasting life...."	Daniel 12:1-2	Not all will be saved See also Revelations 20:13
"And the dust returns to the ground it came from, and the spirit returns to God who gave it."	Ecc. 12:7	Spirit of man; life itself. Physical form is dust; spirit is essence of form.
"Now we know that if the earthly tent we live in is destroyed, we have a building from God, an eternal house in heaven, not built by human hands."	2 Cor. 5:11	A dwelling place in heaven. God's home for us
"In my Father's house are many rooms; if it were not so, I would have told you. I am going there to prepare a place for you."	John 14:2	There is a place for us. Christ prepares the way
"....you will receive a rich welcome into the eternal kingdom of our Lord and Savior Jesus Christ."	2 Peter 1:11	We will be welcomed

God's love for us is reflected in His gifts to us. The gift of His Son for our salvation and His gift to us of eternal life. We need only to accept His gifts.

Milestone #43

Accept God's free gift of eternal life.

1. Do you believe in eternal life? What does eternal life mean to you? How do you describe heaven? Do you believe there is a special place for believers?

2. What happens to unbelievers after their earthly death? Do you believe there is a hell? Explain. Do you believe there is a place between heaven and hell, i.e., purgatory? Explain.

3. When do you believe a child of God is taken to heaven (immediately after death, three days later, second coming of Christ, final judgment, etc.)? Does this pertain to the spiritual body only? Explain.

4. Do you believe that the physical body and spiritual body will be reunited? If so, will the appearance be the same as at the time of death? Explain.

5. Read 1 Thessalonians 4:13-18. What message of resurrection do these verses give you? The second coming of Christ?

6. How do you receive the gift of eternal life? Close in prayer with rejoicing to the Lord and thanksgiving for the free gift of eternal life.

Day of God

Have you ever looked forward to a day or event with great anticipation? Perhaps a special birthday, or a certain gathering, a wedding, or even moreso the birth of a child. We were blessed with two fine, healthy sons. But natural childbirth was no longer an option for Yvonne. It was then that we decided to adopt a child. In that decision, we involved our two sons. We wanted them to share in all aspects of the adoption, from beginning to end.

Generally, in an adoption proceeding, the adoptive parents never really know when the child will arrive into their home. It can happen any day; it can take years. Once a decision is made, the adoptive parents wait with great anticipation for that arrival. They know their joy will be complete with the addition of the child into their home. And so it was with us. We were told it could take as much as two years. This did not diminish our anticipation and watchfulness for that day. The boys were as anxious as we were during this wait.

In actuality, it took only six months, but each actual day of waiting was like a month. Although the day came suddenly, we were prepared. The spare bedroom was made ready as the baby's room. The necessities for caring for an infant were put in place. Clothes were even purchased, although we had no idea what size would be needed.

It was fitting that we first saw her on a Thanksgiving Day. There was much to be thankful for. The next day, our family went to gather that little gem of a girl into our family. The day had finally arrived. It was one of our most memorable days for it was filled with happiness, praise and thanksgiving. It was a time for sharing with family and friends as we joined in fellowship to welcome our new daughter. That night, I wrote the following brief note in Stephanie's baby book:

"God has blessed our family with a binding love for each other. Realizing that sharing our love causes it to get stronger, we found a need to complete our happy family. After a careful review of our needs, we found that a little girl would seemingly best fulfill our needs. Little did we realize that our little girl would be so precious and sweet and lovely. Your need and our need were the same, and that was to share ourselves with each other. Our love for you was so great from the time we started planning for you, and our love continued to grow for you until this very special day. And now that day has come. God has indeed continued his blessings for our loving family. This day is your day. This day is our day. This day is God's day."

Oh that I could live each day on earth as though it were God's day. I am too human to do that. Since Adam, the earthly existence has been the "day of man". The end times will bring us the "day of God".

What will heaven be like? The "New Jerusalem" is just too glorious to imagine (Revelation 21). Paradise will be restored (Revelation 22:1-5). Will we be ready when the Bridegroom comes? (Matthew 25:1-13) Have we prepared ourselves and made ready for the arrival? Are our clothes ready, the lamps filled with oil, the wicks trimmed? When will the Bridegroom come that we may share in the day of God?

As the Bible opens with the story of creation in Genesis, it closes with the promise of life everlasting. A comparison is shown in the following:

DAY OF GOD

"But the day of the Lord will come like a thief.....You ought to live holy and godly lives as you look forward to the <u>day of God</u> and speed its coming.....But in keeping with His promise we are looking forward to a new heaven and a new earth, the home of righteousness." (2 Peter 3:10-13)

Day of Man		Day of God	
Condition	**Reference**	**Condition**	**Reference**
Creation of darkness	Gen 1:3-5	No more night	Rev 22:5
Creation of seas	Gen 1:9-10	No more sea	Rev 21:1
Creation of sun	Gen 1:14-19	No need for the sun	Rev 21:23
Entrance of sin	Gen 3:6	Sin is banished	Rev 21:27
Satan's triumph	Gen 3:13	Satan overthrown	Rev 20:9-10
Pronouncement of curse	Gen 3:14-19	No more death or mourning or crying or pain Curse is gone	Rev 21:4 Rev 22:3
Exclusion from "tree of life"	Gen 3:22-23	Admission to "tree of life"	Rev 22:14

The day of God is at hand. We must prepare ourselves for that day. Jesus tells us (Revelation 22:17), "Whoever is thirsty, let him come; and whoever wishes, let him take the free gift of the water of life." A gift is not a gift until it is accepted by the recipient. My gift is bought and paid for in Jesus; it is there waiting for me; all I need to do is accept it. There is a warning for the gift is not for everyone, as Paul tells us (Romans 6:23), "And the wages of sin is death, but the gift of God is eternal life in Christ Jesus our Lord."

Milestone #44

Be ready for the day of God.

1. Describe an event of great expectation that you experienced. Why was it important to you? How did you prepare for it? How did you feel waiting for the event? Did the event meet your expectations? Explain.

2. Have you ever been to a theme park? Why did you go? Was the monetary cost of travel and admissions a deterrent to make the trip? Why, or why not? Was the use of vacation or free time a deterrent? Do you feel you received full value for your investment of time and money? Explain.

3. What is the most impressive seat of power, or throne, you have seen or read about (1 Kings 10:18-20)? What made this so impressive? Read Revelation 4. Describe your impressions of God's throne. What is the significance of the chorus sung by the four living creatures (v. 8)? By the twenty-four elders (v. 11)?

4. What is the most beautiful place on earth you know of? Why is this place so special to you? Read Revelation 21. Describe your impressions of the New Jerusalem. How does this compare to your special place on earth? How does it compare to your image of heaven?

5. Read Matthew 25:1-13. What is the central theme of this parable? Did the ten virgins appear to be the same? How were they different? Did the ten lamps appear to be the same? How were they different? Why couldn't the unprepared virgins borrow any oil?

6. Do you feel you are ready for the day of God? What can you do to better prepare yourself? How can you help others?

Peace

Faith

Yvonne and I married shortly after graduating from high school, and after two years of, what was then termed as, going steady. It seems we knew from the beginning that we were meant for each other. How could two teenagers know with such certainty that they belonged together? Of course, teenagers know everything! But even this seemed beyond the capability of a teenager.

Over the years we both have been asked that question many times. We have made attempts to answer the question, but I doubt that we really gave a very convincing answer to anyone. It is easy to say all the wonderful attributes I saw in my sweetheart: beauty, charm, gentleness, kindness, humor, love, and the list goes on. It was more than all that. Possibly, it was the wonderful way she responded to me. Certainly what she gave to me was more important then what I could see in her. But it was more than that.

Our forty years of being happily married demonstrates the choice was the right choice, but I am still struggling to answer the question of how could I have known she was the one. My attempt at this answer today is that I sensed what my sweetheart was to be. At that time I couldn't have described it. In reflection, I can only give part of the description. For you see, the dedication to family, support to me, our friendship, her outpouring of love, care and concern are all still growing within her. And each day that love grows more. I couldn't, and didn't, know all that as a teenager. It required a "leap of faith". A leap we both took toward each other. That faith has indeed rewarded me, and each day I love Yvonne more than the day before.

That faith we had, and still have, in each other wasn't just a leap without any following action. Our faith in each other causes us to give ourselves, extend ourselves, to each other and that nurtures our love. It is something that required much work. Attraction to each other can be an instant appeal, but love is an ever-growing, interacting relationship. Basically, it is hard work. We enrich our physical life daily and exercise our bodies for fitness and strength. So too, faith does not grow strong until it is exercised and put into action. Only then will it grow from strength to strength.

The Apostle Paul in his letter to the Hebrews (11:1,6) defines faith as follows: "Now faith is being sure of what we hope for and certain of what we do not see...without faith it is impossible to please God."

God is the Ultimate Truth. I cannot know that truth in this earthly existence. The search for the truth is a continuing journey, an on-going process. What is called fact, or reality, is but our individual perspective of our experience to events. What is called fiction is that which is based on our experience and imagined relationship to events not experienced. Faith is our reaching beyond reality and what is imagined. While tradition and doctrines are a very important part of what I believe, they cannot define my faith. To me, faith is what I am and the knowledge of what I am to become. It is the extension of myself to God and to others.

I used to say that my religion was a personal thing. But I realize now that religion is not personal at all, for it is our expression of our faith. I believe that you cannot be a Christian and be a hermit. These are conflicting concepts. Jesus' teachings of love and service call for us to be involved with others.

There are certain terms that people often use interchangeably that in my mind are very different. Faith, theology, religion, and belief are terms we use in discussing our persuasion. I see them as related terms and the following graphic helps me to explain their relationship:

Faith is our relationship to God
GOD = TRUTH
FAITH = TRUTH

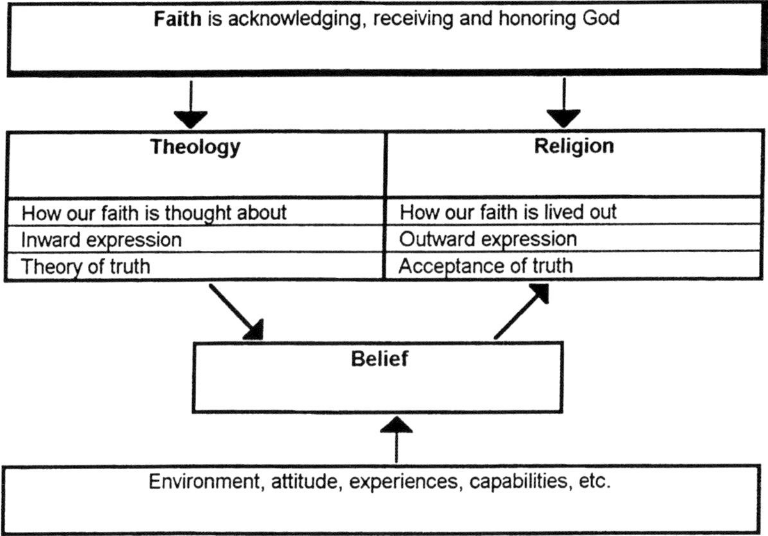

"Faith comes from hearing the message, and the message is heard through the word of Christ." (Romans 10:17).

Faith is a personal relationship with God, but there is nothing personal about it. For faith influences how we think about God and how we live out our religion, and this is our relationship with others. As our faith is strengthened, our love grows. That love will radiate as the spiritual candle, the Holy Ghost, glows within us. When we demonstrate to others that what we have brings contentment, they will want it also.

"Faith by itself, if it's not accompanied by action, is dead." (James 2:17). It is necessary to put our faith to work if we expect to receive the power to make an impact upon the world, but that work is the key to appropriating this power. As Henry Van Dyke put it, "Heaven is blest with rest, but the blessing of earth is toil."

Milestone #45

Take a leap of faith and honor God.

1. Read Luke 2:52; Ephesians 4:14-15. What do you think it means to grow up in all aspects? It can take 100 years for an oak tree to reach its full maturity. List as many factors as you can that contribute to a tree's growth. What do you think are the factors that contribute to spiritual growth?

2. Read 1 Corinthians 3:6-7. Does this have any significance to your personal spiritual growth? Who is the author of that growth?

3. Read 1 Peter 2:1-2; 2 Peter 3:17-18. What are the essentials of spiritual growth? Why are they essential? What areas do you feel you need more knowledge about the Lord?

4. Read Hebrews 5:11-6:2. What are some of the stumbling blocks to spiritual growth? What stumbling blocks have you experienced in your own personal growth?

5. How do you define faith? Do you need to be spiritually mature to have faith? Explain.

6. Do you believe you have faith? If so, what is the basis for that belief? If not, what barriers are preventing you from taking the leap of faith? What would be most helpful to you to nurture your spiritual growth?

Hope

As a youngster my religious exposure was in various Protestant churches. I became very active in the Lutheran church as a teenager and that carried me into manhood. Looking back on that involvement I realized that the Pastor of that particular church was the most significant reason for me remaining in that church. At the time of his death, I was the Lay President of the church. I was very much involved in the search for a new pastor and the transition from the "old" way to the new.

I remember many heated church council meetings where the older members were resisting the changes being brought by the new pastor and his council supporters. Certainly the entire congregation looked on with hope as a young minister took the reins to lead this flock. Everyone was filled with enthusiasm at the possibility of new energy being brought to the church. But that new energy brought about changes that were not welcomed by many. I found myself on one side for a particular issue and on another for some other issue. Then again, I was always considered a maverick, marching along to my own drummer.

From a very early age, I was interested in "religion" and how people lived out their faith. I studied the Bible and read about every religious sect, Christian and non-Christian alike. Many times I found myself in a conversation with someone in another religious sect and realized that I had a basic understanding of their religious background greater than they had. That doesn't speak of any profound knowledge on my part, but rather a lack of understanding of many in even their proclaimed faith. How can that be?

Through the years, Yvonne stood by me and supported my religiosity. She accepted the fact that I was a Lutheran and she was a Catholic, although her family had a problem with that for some years. Our children went to Lutheran Sunday School and Day School as well as attending the liturgy in a Catholic church.

We didn't have conflict in this matter.

For a few years I attended a couple of different Lutheran churches, but never returned to the level of intensity I had in years past. My struggle was that it seemed to me others were going to church for the wrong reasons. People were involved with the activities of the church and focused on the activity. But how was their spirituality being nurtured? I didn't see any signs of it. Suddenly, I came to the realization that it was how I was looking at it. The Pastor that I loved so dearly had been nurturing my spirituality with his own personal involvement with me. Without him I wasn't growing spiritually, nor did I see growth in others because I was measuring them by my own needs. Change was needed. But not in others, as I had thought, but rather in me. But what change?

When I began a new career in Pennsylvania, I was away from Yvonne for most of the time for eight months while our new house was being built. Somewhere early in this separation, I decided that I should attend church services with Yvonne on a regular basis. I called a couple of parishes and explained my desire to attend the liturgy and take communion. Each time I was advised that I had to convert. But one priest said we should talk and discuss the options. I met with the priest and the subject of conversion came up. My response was that there were certain Catholic beliefs that I could not accept. The priest offered to have me go through the instructions and fully explore the differences. So each week for a couple of months, the priest and I met to discuss my understanding and the church's position on many items of doctrine. In the final analysis, there were very few real issues and the priest accepted my view on those and said that I would be welcomed into the Catholic community.

I made the decision to convert. Yvonne knew nothing about this until I scheduled my confirmation. It was quite a surprise to her. Now Yvonne and I enjoy the liturgy together on a regular basis. With my background in Bible study, I can relate the rich tradition of the church to the biblical references. The homily often offers a new understanding, or reinforces an understanding, I have of Christian concepts. I do not always agree with the priest's perspective, but even in that it adds to the nurturing of my spirituality. As I look around the church, I do not see icons, but rather the creative expression of someone's faith. That expression inspires in me a deeper feeling of my faith. As I participate in the liturgy, I do not sense the presentation of dogma, but rather the richness of tradition that is consistent in any Catholic church I happen to attend. As I look around at the community of participants, I do not see the hypocrisy that I once felt, but rather individuals reaching out to be in touch with their God in their own way. It is not that I am more tolerant, but I now understand that each individual is at a different level of spirituality.

The fellowship of the Christian community brings hope to each member. That hope may be somewhat different based on individual need. But the underlying belief in eternal life forms the foundation of that hope. It no longer matters to me what level a person is at in their spiritual growth. How could I ever have thought I was capable of judging that? What matters to me is how I am growing in that spirituality. For me that growth can only come in Christian fellowship, supported by my self-study and reflective thought. This then leads to a reaffirmation of my hope. Hope for myself, hope for others, hope for all of mankind.

Need for Hope

"For everything that was written in the past was written to teach us, so that through endurance and the encouragement of the Scriptures we might have hope." Romans 15:4

Need	Reference	Text
New Birth	1 Peter 1:3	Praise be to the God and Father of our Lord Jesus Christ! In his great mercy he has given us new birth into a living hope through the resurrection of Jesus Christ from the dead.
Saving element of life	Romans 8:24-25	For in this hope we were saved. But hope that is seen is no hope at all, who hopes for what he already has? But if we hope for what we do not yet have, we wait for it patiently.
Purification	1 John 3:3	Everyone who has this hope in him purifies himself, just as he is pure.
Steadfastness	Hebrews 6:18-19	God did this so that, by two unchangeable things in which it is impossible for God to lie, we who have fled to take hold of the hope offered to us may be greatly encouraged. We have this hope as an anchor for the soul, firm and secure.
Testimony	1 Peter 3:15	But in your hearts set apart Christ as Lord. Always be prepared to give an answer to everyone who asks you to give reason for the hope you have. But do this with gentleness and respect.
Refuge in Death	Proverbs 14:32	When calamity comes, the wicked are brought down, but even in death the righteous have a refuge.

As I think of hope, I am reminded of the words of David, "Be strong and take heart, all you who hope in the Lord." (Psalm 31:24) The sacrifice of Christ for my sins reminds me that there is nothing in this world that can take away that cleansing. The promise of everlasting life given by my Lord gives me the optimism to look forward to a better tomorrow. The resurrection of Jesus, gives me the assurance that death will be conquered.

Each day I pray that I be refilled with the Holy Spirit for I know the day before I made decisions that caused some to spill out. I know that I will be blessed with that refilling. The Holy Spirit guides me each day, and provides me with the hope of that day and all of the tomorrows. I do not know what is coming, but I know that, ultimately, I will be in the heavenly kingdom and it will be more glorious and beautiful than I can ever imagine. I have that hope.

Milestone #46

Put your hope in the Lord and He will not disappoint you.

1. Have you had a recent experience where you hoped for something? Explain. What action, if any, was required on your part for this to happen? Where you fully, or partially, dependent on action from some other person? Explain.

2. How do you define hope? Does your definition apply to spiritual hope? If not, how does it differ?

3. Read Romans 5:1-5. Does this passage give you a personal message of justification? Peace? Hope? Explain each.

4. Why is there a need for hope? Do you have hope? What impact does spiritual hope have on your daily life?

5. In the chart, Need for Hope, a progression of need is implied. Where are you in that progression? What area of need do you feel you require further understanding of hope? Why? What can you do to get that understanding?

6. Read Titus 3:4-7. Offer a prayer of thanksgiving to God for the hope of eternal life you have.

Love

Several years ago Stephanie was having difficulty in maintaining friendships. After some discussion, I told her the following:

"From my view, you have selected 'takers' instead of 'givers' for your friends. The extended hand of a taker is not the same as the extended hand of the giver. The taker's hand can give warmth and a sense of security as it grasps you. In time, that grasp can become a strangle hold and the grip must be abruptly broken. If broken by the taker, it is only because there is nothing left to take. The extended hand of the giver, however, does not necessarily give warmth through the grasp. Rather, it is always there, within reach, for you to take hold of in time of need. The comfort is in knowing that the hand is always there. It takes more time to learn to trust in the presence rather than the grasp. But in that time, true friendship develops. As a giver gives to you and you give to the giver, it creates an attitude of sharing and this is what friendship is about. Begin by letting Jesus be your friend. You will find strength in that friendship and He will lead you to others who will be true friends to you. There are many givers who would want to be your friend."

In his book, "The Road Less Traveled," M. Scott Peck writes, "Love is the willing extension of oneself that nurtures the spiritual growth of yourself or others." Love is a giving attitude. To love others though, we must first love ourselves. The Apostle Matthew (22:39) writes, "Love your neighbor as yourself."

The answer for peace and joy in this world is love. In years passed, I wondered about the limitations of God's love. There are so many people. Could He possible love them all? Before my grandson was born, I felt that I could not possibly love another more than my wife and children. But after the birth of Ryan, I found I loved him more than I thought I possibly could. Even more astounding to me, I found that I actually loved my sons more, my daughter more, my wife more. In fact my capacity for love seemed to have grown on an exponential scale. Then I realized God's secret: The more you love, the more capacity you have for love. This theory was tested again when Sarah Anne, and later Taylor, was born. God has put no limit on our ability to love. Surely, God's capacity to love is unending.

The chain of love is one that begins with God's love for us. We must respond to Him with love. From that we are filled with the unlimited capacity to love others. Each step in the love process brings us closer to that pure, unlimited love.

THE LOVE PROCESS

"He who pursues righteousness and love finds life, prosperity and honor."
(Prov. 21:21)

Process Steps	Reference	Text
God's love	Psalm 25:6,7	Remember, O Lord, your great mercy and love, for they are from old. Remember not the sins of my youth and my rebellious ways; according to your love remember me.....
	Psalm 66:20	Praise be to God, who has not rejected my prayer or withheld his love from me.
	Romans 5:8	But God demonstrates his own love for us in this: While we were still sinners, Christ died for us.
	1 John 3:1	How great is the love the Father has lavished on us, that we should be called children of God! And that is what we are!
Love of God	Deut. 6:5	Love the Lord your God with all your heart and with all your soul and with all your strength.
	1 Chron. 16:34	Give thanks to the Lord, for he is good; his love endures forever.
	Matthew 22:37	Jesus replied: "Love the Lord your God with all your heart and with all your soul and with all your mind.
	2 John 1:6	And this is love: that we walk in obedience to his commands. As you have heard from the beginning, his command is that you walk in love.
Love others	Matthew 5:44	But I tell you: Love your enemies and pray for those who persecute you.
	Ephesians 5:1-2	Be imitators of God, therefore, as dearly beloved children and live a life of love...
	1 Peter 4:8	Above all, love each other deeply, because love covers over a multitude of sins.
	1 John 4:12	No one has ever seen God; but if we love one another, god lives in us and his love is made complete in us.
Progression	2 Peter 1:5-7	For this very reason, make every effort to add to your faith goodness; and to goodness, knowledge; and to knowledge, self-control; and to self-control, perseverance; and to perseverance, godliness; and to godliness, brotherly kindness; and to brotherly kindness, love.
Attributes	1 Corinth. 13:4-8	Love is patient, love is kind. It does not envy, it does not boast, it is not proud. It is not rude, it is not self-seeking, it is not easily angered, it keeps no record of wrongs. Love does not delight in evil but rejoices with the truth. It always protects, always trusts, always hopes, always perseveres. Love never fails....

As I review what I call the love process, I see a growth pattern that has its beginning with the Creator. God first loves, as a parent loves a child. Then the child loves in response, which is our love of God. This teaches us to love others from the example given to us by God. "This is how we know that we love the children of God: by loving God and carrying out his commands. This is love for God: to obey his commands. And his commands are not burdensome." (1 John 5:2-3). Indeed His commands are not burdensome. Jesus advised us to first love God the Father and then to love one another (Matthew 22:34-40). Love is such an all encompassing word that it is sometimes difficult to define. The steps taken in the process to love and the attributes evident in love help us to better understand it. The more we love, the greater knowledge of love we have.

The essence of our responsive love, as a child loves a parent, is trust or faith. Then it progresses to maturing stages of love: goodness, knowledge, self-control, perseverance, godliness, brotherly kindness, and ultimately, pure love. Where am I along this progression? I know that as I progress through these maturing stages I am becoming more Christlike, more like the person God wants me to be.

Then I look at the attributes of love and ask if I truly display those qualities. If a sincere and pure love is within me then these qualities will be evident. Only true love will keep me consistently in those qualities. It is easy enough to pretend, for awhile, to be loving. One can even say that they display one or more of the traits of love all the time. But the pure and true love demonstrates all these traits all the time. Certainly I fall short of this. It is a goal that one must reach for to attain. It is an on-going process, a plan for continual improvement. For I know that "Love never fails".

Milestone #47

Love others through God's love of you.

1. Can you identify one person you love more than anyone else? If so, why is this love so special? If not, is there a group of individuals you can identify? Why is this love so special?

2. There is the golden rule, "Do unto others as you would have them do unto you!" There is also the platinum rule, "Treat others as they want to be treated!" What is the difference in these two statements? Which rule is easier to follow? Why?

3. What does it mean to "love your neighbors as ourselves!"? How do you demonstrate this rule? Do you believe you follow this rule? What are the enablers to you? What are the barriers?

4. Spend a few minutes reviewing the chart, The Love Process. List in one column the attributes that are included in love and in another column the attributes that do not reflect love.

5. Is it possible to show love to someone with whom you are angry? Someone you dislike? A stranger? If so, how is this love demonstrated? If not, should you? Is it possible to love things? Is so, how is this demonstrated?

6. How do you define love? Do you love God? How do you demonstrate this? Do you feel there are different levels of love? Explain.

The Eternal Circle

I have been a sports enthusiast for most of my life. As a youngster I collected baseball cards. Unfortunately, I didn't have the foresight to maintain and safeguard that collection. I remember from a very early age, that my father played industrial league baseball. Some years later, in my late teens, my father invited me to play with him. That was quite an event for me. It had been a long-time hope that I would someday be good enough to play baseball with him. Also, it gave the message that he had faith in me to be able to bring value to the team. I never told him of my youthful hope; yet, he asked me to share this with him. What a happy time it was for me to be on the same team as my father.

We played together for several years. When he felt that he had lost too much of his speed, I went with him to a softball league. Those spring and summer evenings still race through my mind. During this time, I got married and started a family of my own. I remember when Bruce, and later Michael, was born and I silently promised that I would participate in sports with him.

Dad dropped out of softball, but I continued in baseball, softball and basketball. As soon as Bruce was old enough to hold a little plastic bat, about two years old, I had him in the back yard pitching to him and having him catch the ball. It was a lot harder work than I expected. I worked individually with Bruce and Michael in the skills of baseball, football and basketball until they joined little league and school teams. Then I participated by coaching little league. This made for a very hectic life at home. We were always eating on the run, and rushing off here and there for one game or another. But I loved every moment of it.

Throughout all of this, my sons and I shared with my father our enthusiasm for the Baltimore Colts and the Baltimore Orioles. The years slipped by; the activity stopped; we all went our separate ways. Surely, it was a gradual transition, but it seemed to have just come to a sudden halt. A memory though rises out of the past and rekindles the excitement I experienced with our shared participation in sports.

My father, Bruce, Michael and myself were able to attend the fifth, and final, game of the 1983 World Series in Baltimore between our beloved Orioles and the Philadelphia Phillies. We had a grand time, a fun time. Our shared participation was in the role of spectators, but it was all the more sweet because I was with my father and my sons. With the Orioles winning the game, and the series, it made the day that much more enjoyable.

As I relive that event, I have often thought of my life coming full circle. The flashback of my hope to someday play baseball with my father and then have that hope fulfilled through his faith in me; the desire to participate with my sons and then taking the effort to make that happen; the occasion that brought three generations of Johnson "boys" together for a day of fun-loving fellowship. Each thought, each comment, each action of the occasion brought back memories from the past. My hope for tomorrow, the hopes of my sons; my father's faith in me; my faith in my sons. All of this bonded together in the love we have for each other. My father extended himself to me. In return, I extended myself to him and later to my sons. They in turn, extended themselves to me and their Grandfather. It was not three separate levels of manhood enjoying that game, but a connected chain, a circle, a unity found in oneness.

And the unity continues. It is now ten years later. I look around to see again three generations of Johnson boys together at a ballgame in the new Oriole Park. But the roles we play are now different. I am the grandfather; Bruce is a father-to-be; Michael is the father, and Ryan has joined us as the son. The event is rich in enjoyment because of the memory of yesterday. The unbroken chain intact; the circle complete.

There are three attributes so closely tied to each other that I see them in a continuous circle; one that I call The Eternal Circle.

THE ETERNAL CIRCLE
A formula for being in harmony with God.

"So faith, hope, love abide; these three but the greatest of these is love." (1 Cor. 13:13)

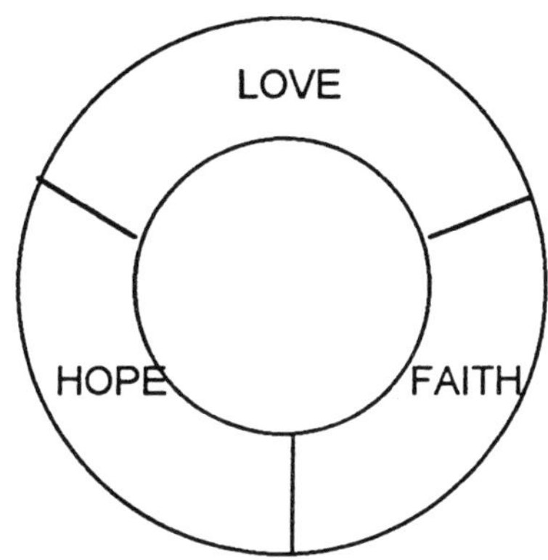

With a firm Faith there is Hope for tomorrow.

With Hope for tomorrow there is Love today.

With Love today there is a Faith everlasting.

The constant interaction of these attributes strengthens each of them. The combined strength of them nurtures my growth. I am what I am to be! Today's self and yesterday's self had within them the potential for tomorrow's self.

Milestone #48

Live a life of faith, filled with hope, that leads to love for all.

1. Read 2 Peter 1:5-9. What qualities of faith are mentioned in this passage? Can you identify other qualities in an individual that reflect their faith? Which attributes are qualities of attitude and which are qualities of action? What is the result of faith?

2. Read Philippians 2:1-17. What qualities of hope can you identify in this passage? Are there other qualities in an individual that reflect their hope? Which of these qualities reinforces the hope within the individual? Which reinforces the hope in others?

3. Take a few minutes to list all the qualities of love that come to mind. Which of these attributes are qualities of attitude and which are qualities of action? Which are qualities reflected in love of oneself and which are reflected in love of others? Must an individual love themselves before they can love others? Explain.

4. What does the symbol of the circle mean to you? How would you describe your circle of friends? Is this a limited group or an extended group? How do you interact with each other?

5. How do you see faith impacting hope and love? Hope impacting faith and love? Love impacting faith and hope? Can there be one without the other?

6. Read 1 Corinthians 13. What message does this passage give you personally? Is there any change you must make in your life to be in harmony with the eternal circle of faith, hope and love? Explain.

Assurances

Yvonne's brother, Frank, graduated from the Marine Corps boot camp when our sons were at a very impressionable age. For the graduation ceremonies, the family took the long drive from Maryland to Parris Island, South Carolina. It rained for most of the long, grueling drive, but we arrived safely about 3:00 a.m. on the morning of the ceremony. It seemed that we were in bed barely long enough to wrinkle the sheets when it was time to get up and make the trip to the Marine base for the early morning parade. It was an unusually cold, December day. Marines were busy serving coffee and blankets to the arriving spectators. If anyone would spill any coffee, it immediately froze on the bleacher seats. Yvonne and I decided to park the car as close to the parade grounds as possible and let Bruce and Michael watch from the relative warmth of the car. Bruce was eight years old and Michael was four, so I stood near the car to keep a watch on them. To me, all United States military ceremonies are inspiring as emotions of loyalty, pride and love swell up within me. This one was no exception. The fact that my brother-in-law was participating made the emotions all the more intense.

It wasn't until years later that I found out it had a significant impact on Michael. He told his mother and me that it was then he knew he would go into the military. That impression stayed with him and formed a desire, at an early age, to attend the Naval Academy. Michael knew he was going to be a graduate of the Academy.

As Michael neared graduation from high school, he stood near the top of his class in academics and was acclaimed as one of the outstanding track and field athletes in the country. His SAT scores were well over the required minimum for entrance to the Academy. Yvonne and I worked at obtaining the necessary political endorsements. About 13,000 applicants were seeking to fill the 1,100 appointments that would be made that year. Michael was confident, as we all were, that he would indeed get an appointment.

This happened to be the first year of eligibility for females. The Navy was required to fill the plebe class with 110 young women. As it turned out, Michael lost his appointment to one of these women. He was devastated, and we all hurt for him and with him. Michael had gone through the motions of submitting applications to other colleges and universities. Now he was faced with the decision of whether to pursue one of these acceptances and lose a dream, or find another answer to being accepted at the Academy.

Michael, Yvonne and I worked together to develop all the possible options. Following every lead and talking to as many people as possible, we were eventually introduced to the Director of the Naval Academy Alumni Association. He researched Michael's background and advised us that Michael was the type of young man the Academy wanted, and went on to advise us that the Alumni Association would sponsor Michael, but he would have to attend a preparatory school of their choosing for a year and then reapply for the Academy through normal channels the next year. It was then we learned that Michael's verbal score on his SAT is what kept him in the lower 10% of possible appointees. It wasn't the young women that kept him out of the Academy, but rather his understanding of the English language.

Anger changed to determination as Michael decided he would go to the Academy the next year and accepted the conditions by going to a military type preparatory school. A large portion of Michael's curriculum for that year was related to English, at the direction of the Alumni Association. The disappointment from one year led to the success of the next year. Michael's SAT verbal scores climbed 100 points, he was a stand-out student, athlete and leader. And yes, an appointee to the Naval Academy.

This was possible because Michael knew he was going to graduate from the Academy. The timing wasn't exactly as planned; the assurance was shaken somewhat; the temptation to move in another direction was strong. But the overwhelming knowledge that he was meant to go to the Naval Academy won out. In knowing that, he was able to actuate the happening. I believe he would be the first to admit that he could not have done it alone, without the support of all those who love him. This in no way takes away from the effort that Michael, himself, put into making a dream a reality.

I see in this, an assurance tested. Michael, and me as well, could easily blame some outside influence that took away the assurance, such as, women being admitted into the Academy. Then Michael had to feel that he failed himself and questioned his own confidence. But then the realization that the real cause was just one of working a little harder on certain skills. Once the fog lifts; once your support mechanism is in place, such as family and friends; once your confidence returns, you can move forward with the full measure of assurance of what lies before you.

We move through life with confidence when we have assurances for what lies ahead. And doesn't life test us by challenging those things, and people, that we placed our assurance in? As time goes on, aren't we inclined to stop believing in those assurances? And as our assurances drift away, don't we lose the confidence in ourselves, in life itself? A certainty of yesterday, even though now hidden, can be returned to certainty for today and then for tomorrow.

The key element in determining that one is a Christian is to recognize that Jesus is the Savior. Like the Samaritans, we can profess, "We no longer believe just because of what you said; now we have heard for ourselves, and we know that this man really is the Savior of the world." (John 4:42)

Once I heard the words of Christ and the supporting comments from His disciples and followers, I could do no other than accept Him as my Savior. By doing that I have found growing confidence in that faith. The following table reflects the assurances all believers can have:

CERTAINTIES OF FAITH
What the Believer can know

"We know that we have come to know him if we obey his commands.....if anyone obeys his word, God's love is truly made complete in him. This is how we know we are in him: Whoever claims to live in him must walk as Jesus did." (1 John 2:3-6)

Assurance that:	Reference	Text
My Redeemer lives	Job 19:25	"I know that my redeemer lives, and that in the end he will stand upon the earth."
Reverence to God brings knowledge	Proverbs 1:7	"The fear of the Lord is the beginning of knowledge."
God works for the good of believers	Romans 8:28	"And we know that in all things God works for the good of those who love him, who have been called according to his purpose."
Righteous life indicates regeneration	1 John 2:29	"....you know that everyone who does what is right has been born of him."
We shall be like Christ at His coming	1 John 3:2	"....we know that when he appears, we shall be like him, for we shall see him as his is."
Christ came to take away sin	1 John 3:5	"But you know that he appeared so that he might take away our sin, for in him is no sin."
Brotherly love brings us to life	1 John 3:14	"We know that we have passed from death to life, because we love our brothers...."
Christ lives in us through the Spirit	1 John 3:24	"And this is how we know he lives in us: We know it by the Spirit he gave us."
We have eternal life	1 John 5:13	"I write these things to you who believe in the name of the Son of God so that you may know that you have eternal life."
Our prayers will be answered	1 John 5:15	"And if we know he hears us - whatever we ask - we know that we have what we asked of him."

God provides this spiritual knowledge to His chosen. Filled with this knowledge I have the further knowledge that I am known by God. "But the man who loves God, is known by God." (1 Corinthians 8:3) "The Lord knows those who are his." (2 Timothy 2:19)

Milestone #49

Have confidence in your faith.

1. What are you most sure of in your life (home, work, community, environment, church, etc.)? Why are you so certain of this? What is your confidence level of certainty? If less than 100%, what causes any doubt of certainty? How could you increase your level of confidence?

2. It is often said that the only things in life we can be certain of are taxes and death. Do you agree with this statement? Explain.

3. Read 2 Corinthians 5:1-10. What assurances do you find in these verses? What does this passage say about the certainties of our earthly existence? What does it say of mortality?

4. Review the chart, Certainties of Faith. How certain are you of each of the assurances listed? Which of them are you most certain? Which least certain? What evidence do you feel you need to increase your level of confidence in any one of these?

5. If you were to die today, how certain are you that you will achieve eternal life in God's heavenly kingdom? Explain. What must you do, if anything, to achieve 100% confidence in this?

6. Do you have confidence to discuss your faith with others? Does a Bible study group give you greater confidence to discuss your faith? Why? What barriers are there in discussing your faith with members of your family? Your friends and acquaintances? Strangers? What can you do to increase your confidence level in discussing your faith?

Conclusion

The Journey Continues

I have noticed that if you drive through a fog, you can look back through the rear-view mirror and see clearly the road behind you. But yet the road ahead is barely visible. The moment we experienced the passage, all around us was clouded, filled with shadowy images. The lights before us seem so far distant. Our previous experiences gave us the mind's eye view of that moment. Now, as we look back through our rear-view mirror, we see that much of the imagined view was accurate, but much was not. Having passed that moment though, we are now better prepared to go forward through the fog. Our perceptions and anticipations are keener because of what we now see in the rear-view mirror.

All of this earthly existence is like that brief trip through the fog. We do not, and cannot, know what is before us. But each past moment of our journey can bring us a better vision of the moment we are experiencing. How we react to this experience can better prepare us for the distant light that comes ever closer. As we approach the light, the light approaches us.

Some twenty-five years ago I had ideals that surprise me today. Was it youthful idealism or an internal truth that I lost grasp of for awhile? Let me share with you a verse I wrote those many years ago.

My Temple to God

I will build a temple to Thee, O God;
But not one with a large and gleaming facade.
Nor will it have towering, radiant spires,
Nor lofts filled with gospel singing choirs.
No, not a structure visible to the eye
That inspires with awe the people that pass by.

My humble edifice is destined to be
No more than a cornerstone laid for Thee.
And the tools required for this meager construction
Are nothing more than the talents which Thou has given.
The most precious of materials will I choose,
Which is the time allotted on earth for me to use.

Each day I'll set at the task of building
By showing interest, concern and love in sharing
With all persons, the blessings of my heritage.
And I'll strive to always present the good image
That my children will follow and be proud of,
And learn from it the meaning of brotherly love.

I'll strive to improve myself and then endeavor
To work for the benefit of my family and neighbor.
Knowing full well, recognition is not mine to achieve,
I'll continue to work with rolled-up sleeves.
And when my allotted working days come to an end,
The task will be left to others to continue the trend.

The temple built for Thee cannot possibly be
Completed by anyone as small as me.
But in knowing that I have placed the cornerstone,
My family, friends and neighbors can go on
And construct a tabernacle so large and grand,
Because it will be made of love with helping hands.

My life indeed has been a roller-coaster ride as I fell into the pot-holes of life. I did not clearly see the milestones and street signs along much of the way. With a rekindled fire in my faith, I have achieved a level of peace and happiness that had been absent from my life for a very long time. I have taken time to look into my rear-view mirror to better understand where I have been. I am prepared to adjust my way as I continue my search for the Ultimate Truth. It seems I am now growing into those dreams and ideals of that young adult.

I now invite Jesus to guide me in my daily choices. There is a level of peace and joy and understanding that grows within me each day. Through the Holy Spirit, God is working with me in my spiritual growth. And I know that God is not finished with me yet!

The Spiritual Highway

Our family has always traveled together along the road of life. We were there for each other and ever anxious to help. Each of us had periods in our lives that we focused inwardly and drifted from the path of the others. Each of us have returned to the Johnson caravan to continue the journey together. We are more open with each other than we ever have been. The journey for each of us has been difficult in its own way. The journey of the family has been difficult. Yet I know if we had not made the journey together, it would have been all the more treacherous.

Our road in this life has led us to a superhighway. A highway that we all are committed to travel upon. It is the highway that nurtures our spiritual growth. It is a journey toward the truth.

The road we traveled in our daily life has at times run parallel to the spiritual highway; sometimes it intersected and headed off in another direction. Each parting left us lost in worldly concerns and despair, and each return brought us peace and joy. Now I see that the road of life and the spiritual highway can be shared roadways. They can be, and must be traveled together. The spiritual highway will carry you along the road of life if you follow the Light along the way.

The Spiritual Highway

"Set up road signs; put up guideposts. Take note of the highway, the road you take." (Jeremiah 31:21)

Condition	Reference	Text
Name	Isaiah 35:8	And a highway will be there; it will be called the Way of Holiness. The unclean will not journey on it; it will be for those who walk in that Way; wicked fools will not go about on it.
Increase understanding	Proverbs 4:18	The path of the righteous is like the first gleam of dawn, shining ever brighter till the full light of day.
Limited access	Matthew 7:14	But small is the gate and narrow the road that leads to life, and a few find it.
Rules of conduct	Proverbs 4:25-27	Let your eyes look straight ahead, fix your gaze directly before you. Make level paths for your feet and take only ways that are firm. Do not swerve to the right or the left; keep your feet from evil.
Warning	Proverbs 21:16	A man who strays from the path of understanding comes to rest in the company of the dead.

The effort of this book has been to place road signs and guide-posts along the spiritual highway so that others may notice and contemplate the message at each stopping place. The attempt is to share the experience of a family and their perspective of a trip they have been traveling. If but one of the road signs causes you to pause for just a little while, then our journey, our road map, has served its purpose.

Milestone #50

Continue your journey along the spiritual highway.

1. What is the most memorable trip you have taken? How did you prepare for the trip? Were others involved in making the arrangements or preparing for the trip? How? What were your expectations for completing the trip?

2. Were the results of the trip as you expected? Explain. In what ways have you attempted to retain the memory of the experience (souvenirs, photographs, trip log, etc.)? Would you make that trip again? Why, or why not?

3. Have you ever returned to visit a place that you once enjoyed? Was the trip as enjoyable as the first trip? Did everything seem the same to you? If different, how? What new experiences, if any, did you have?

4. Have you ever stopped along a highway to read a historical marker? Did you feel you wanted to know more about the event, place or person noted in the marker? What ways could you find out more about the event, place or person?

5. What does spiritual growth mean to you? Do you believe you are experiencing spiritual growth? What are the barriers? Is reading the Bible the only way to gain understanding of God? Explain. Have you ever reread a Bible passage and gained a different understanding of the passage? What will you do in the next three months to improve your understanding of God?

6. Spend a few minutes praying for wisdom and understanding to ways of God. Ask for an awareness of God's will in your life and to lead you along the righteous way.

Your Journey is Yours

The course has been set with the rules and instructions that span thousands of years. Our destination has been gloriously defined. You are invited to follow the spiritual highway and enjoy the beauty and majesty of this life along the way. Some of the resting places are noted in this road map. There are many others for you to find on your own.

As you make your journey, do not eagerly set expectations without first asking God to set His expectations of you within your heart. Where we travel, what we get out of our earthly existence should not be from our expectations, but rather from the will of God. It is His expectations in our life that really matter. He is most willing to guide you along your journey. Success of the journey has already been assured through Jesus Christ.

The trials and tribulations that some have may not be avoided, but God provides a way through all of this. He is with you on your journey. While you may not realize His presence, He is always there. Each step of the way He supports, comforts, and lifts you up. He encourages you constantly to draw near to Him, to take the next step along the way. Your road of life, even along the Spiritual Highway, may be difficult for you. But with God's help, it will be made worthwhile. "Those who hope in the Lord will renew their strength. They will soar on wings like eagles; they will run and not grow weary, they will walk and not be faint." (Isaiah 40:31)

The journey is a journey that continues through eternity. Your journey is yours alone to make. It is a journey in faith. As you proceed toward the destination, God, in a time of His choosing will say to you, "I carried you on eagles' wings and brought you to myself." (Exodus 19:4)

"I want to know Christ and the power of his resurrection and the fellowship of sharing in his sufferings, becoming like him in his death, and so, somehow, to attain to the resurrection from the dead. Not that I have already obtained all this, or have already been made perfect, but I press on to take hold of that for which Christ Jesus took hold of me."

Philippians 3:10-12